# With Heroic Truth

## The Life of
## Edward R. Murrow

# With Heroic Truth

## The Life of Edward R. Murrow

*by Norman H. Finkelstein*

Clarion Books

*New York*

Clarion Books
a Houghton Mifflin Company imprint
215 Park Avenue South, New York, NY 10003
Text copyright © 1997 by Norman H. Finkelstein

Type is 13.25 Dante.
Book design by Carol Goldenberg.

Library of Congress Cataloging-in-Publication Data
Finkelstein, Norman H.
 With heroic truth : the life of Edward R. Murrow / by Norman H. Finkelstein.
 p.  cm.
 Includes bibliographical references and index.
 ISBN 0-395-67891-9
 1. Murrow, Edward R.—Juvenile literature.  2. Journalists—United States—
Biography—Juvenile literature.  3. Radio journalists—United States—Biography—
Juvenile literature.  4. Television journalists—United States—Biography—Juvenile
literature.[1. Murrow, Edward R.  2. Journalists.]  I. Title.
PN4874.M89F56   1997   070'.92—dc20
[B]                94-25128
                         CIP
                          AC

HOR  10  9  8  7  6  5  4  3  2  1

FRONTISPIECE: *Murrow on* See It Now *set, 1952 (WSU)*

*For Robert and Risa*

# Acknowledgments

The author extends grateful appreciation to the Estate of Edward R. Murrow for permission to quote from the broadcast transcripts of Edward R. Murrow; the Murrow Collection at the Fletcher School of Law and Diplomacy, Tufts University, Medford, Massachusetts; the Manuscripts, Archives, and Special Collections Department of Washington State University, Pullman, Washington; the CBS News Reference Library, New York, and its director, Laura Kapnick; the CBS Broadcast Group and the director of photo operations, Martin Silverstein; Dan Rather and Charles Kuralt, CBS News, for permission to quote from published writings and personal correspondence to the author.

My thanks also go to the staffs of: the Museum of Television and Radio, New York; the John F. Kennedy Presidential Library, Boston; the National Archives and the Library of Congress, Washington; and the Library of Hebrew College,

Brookline, Massachusetts, Maurice Tuchman, Director. I owe special gratitude to my wife, Rosalind, for her continued support and understanding.

The author particularly appreciates the gracious hospitality and cooperation of Janet H. B. Murrow and Casey Murrow. Their reminiscences enrich this book with revealing personal glimpses of Edward R. Murrow.

# Contents

Prologue · xi

1. The Reporter and the Senator · 1
2. From Polecat Creek to Pullman · 19
3. The Student Prince · 29
4. A Fateful Phone Call · 43
5. Eyewitness to History · 53
6. This . . . Is London · 65
   A Photographic Portfolio · 81
7. Orchestrated Hell · 101
8. See It Now: Television News · 117
9. Off Camera · 133
10. The Bureaucrat · 147
    Epilogue: Good Night and Good Luck · 161
    Bibliography · 165
    Research Notes · 167
    Index · 169

*Murrow recording album (National Archives)*

# Prologue

The spacious reception lobby of the CBS Broadcast Center on West Fifty-Seventh Street in New York City bustles with businesslike activity. Visitors, employees, and celebrities continually come and go. The walls of the lobby are plain, largely unadorned by paintings, signs, or photographs. The only exception is a small plaque, permanently attached to the wall closest to the entrance. Most people pass it by without notice. For some who do stop and read, it seems almost out of place. The words do not extol the Columbia Broadcasting System, its principles, or its founder, William Paley. Instead, they pay tribute to an individual, dead since 1965, who never worked in that building but whose spirit hovers above every news broadcast produced there. It reads:

Edward R. Murrow's untimely death deprives our country of one of its most dedicated and eloquent spokesmen. The people of the free world are deeply in his debt. So is broadcast journalism which, in so many ways, he helped to establish and of which he was one of the finest practitioners. He set standards of excellence that remain unsurpassed. His thoughtful spirit of inquiry, his profound insight and his single-minded devotion to quality were without parallel in radio, television or any other medium. His imprint on broadcasting will be felt for all time to come. The history of the many years during which he was associated with the Columbia Broadcasting System as reporter, executive, as member of the Board, spans in large measure the history of broadcast journalism in general and of CBS News in particular.

*The words of Ed Murrow speak for themselves. Spare and lean as the man himself, referred to by many as prose poetry. These words form an anthology of our time.*

—CBS News Reporter Robert Trout
April 30, 1965

# With Heroic Truth

The Life of
Edward R. Murrow

*McCarthy at microphones, 1954 (Library of Congress)*

# CHAPTER ONE

# The Reporter and the Senator

*We cannot defend freedom abroad by deserting it at home.*
                              —Edward R. Murrow

Readers of *The New York Times* on March 9, 1954, were puzzled by the simple advertisement tucked away on a back page. "Tonight at 10:30 on *See It Now*, a report on Senator Joseph R. McCarthy over channel 2." It was signed simply, "Fred W. Friendly, Edward R. Murrow, co-producers." Missing was any indication that the program would be aired over the Columbia Broadcasting System. Even the familiar CBS "eye" logo was absent. The newspaper readers did not know that CBS refused to advertise this specific *See It Now* program. At the last moment, Friendly and Murrow had reached into their own pockets to pay for the advertisement.

At the CBS studios, extra security guards stood outside the control room as the seasoned staff of technicians prepared for the 10:30 P.M. broadcast. This program had to be perfect. *See It Now*, hosted by Edward R. Murrow, had been on the air for three years. Still, every live program had its own needs. Film clips had to be timed to the second and the script carefully structured.

The previous fall, Murrow twice reported on the climate of political fear rampant in 1950s America. The first program was about a young air force officer, Milo Radulovich. He was being forced to resign his commission because of allegations that his father and sister were disloyal to the United States. The second program focused on a community debate in Indianapolis about the right of the American Civil Liberties Union to rent a meeting hall.

Ed Murrow was no beginner. He had coinvented *See It Now* when he was already a broadcasting legend, and gained even more fame as the program's on-air host. Yet, even he felt the nervous tension as airtime for this third program approached. That afternoon, in an unusual but appreciated gesture, the founder of CBS, William Paley, called to offer his support.

At precisely 10:30 P.M., the rousing orchestral theme of the *See It Now* series introduced the program. Murrow stared up into a slightly elevated camera, positioned for ultimate visual effect, and began to speak in his deep, familiar, authoritative voice. "Good evening," he intoned. "Tonight, *See It Now* devotes its entire half hour to a report on Senator Joseph R. McCarthy, told mainly in his own words and pictures." For the next thirty minutes, viewers sat transfixed before their televisions as the meteoric political career of the junior senator from Wisconsin began to self-destruct.

Few figures in United States history have left their names to a political style or movement. Today, the highly charged term "McCarthyism" lives on to describe the use of reckless, unproven accusations of disloyalty against an individual. McCarthy was largely a product of his time. Following World War II, the United States was engaged in a "Cold War" with its former wartime ally the Soviet Union. Hostility between the two nations dated back to the 1917 Communist Revolution due to the longstanding threats of world revolution by the Communist leaders of the Soviet Union.

As Americans looked on with apprehension, Communists experienced one success after another in the late 1940s and early 1950s. In 1949, Communist revolutionaries in China successfully overthrew the existing government, which had been an ally of the United States. That same year, the Soviet Union jolted the world by announcing possession of an atomic bomb, thereby joining the United States as the world's only other nuclear power. Relations between the two superpowers worsened. At his inauguration in 1953, President Dwight David Eisenhower said, "Forces of good and evil are massed and armed. . . . Freedom is pitted against slavery, lightness against dark."

Fear and disbelief gripped America. The red flags of Communism seemed to flutter across the globe. How could the Soviets have attained such power so quickly after the devastation they suffered during World War II? How did they gain the knowledge to become a nuclear power?

Many thought the Soviet Union could only have achieved such advances with help from American traitors. There had always been official espionage on both sides, but now, anti-Communism in the United States exploded into paranoid fear of the Soviet Union and of Communists taking over the United States by force or subversion.

In Congress, the House Un-American Activities Committee (HUAC) swung into gear to expose alleged pro-Communist activities within the government and important industries. A particularly popular target, in light of a string of diplomatic failures, was the United States State Department.

In 1947, President Harry Truman instituted a loyalty oath for employees of the federal government. Politicians took advantage of the climate of irrational fear to paint their opponents as "Reds," "pinkos," or "Commies." In 1950, the Internal Security Act, sometimes referred to as the McCarran Act, instituted regulations for rooting out alleged Communists and their sympathizers from the United States government.

While the business of selling and building bomb shelters flourished, Americans were treated to an increasing number of "anti-Red" films at their local movie houses. Titles such as *I Was a Communist for the FBI, I Married a Communist,* and *The Red Menace* helped fuel a condition of near mass hysteria. Bubble gum trading cards taught children to "fight the Red menace" by joining the "Children's Crusade Against Communism." In the minds of many Americans, Communists and traitors lurked everywhere. The search for Communist sympathizers was relentless. People simply accused of liberal views lost their jobs or were "blacklisted" from other positions. Many Americans tragically discovered that rights granted them under the Constitution of the United States could not protect them from the self-righteous, rabid "Commie" hunters to whom a false accusation or malicious rumor was taken as a sign of certain guilt.

In 1950, the junior senator from Wisconsin stumbled into this emotionally charged atmosphere by "discovering" the political power of anti-Communism. Joseph R. McCarthy—he preferred to be known simply as Joe—was a circuit court judge before entering the marines in 1942. His first election to public office was memorable only because his advertisements falsely added twenty years to the age of his opponent, allowing Joe to run as the "youth" candidate.

As a marine officer during World War II, he never fired a shot in battle. His goal was to survive the war and return home to seek election to the United States Senate. He used every opportunity to send inflated stories home to local newspapers about his "enhanced" wartime activities. Pictures and stories of brave "tail gunner Joe," the self-proclaimed battle-hardened survivor of dangerous enemy missions, appeared in newspapers all over Wisconsin. When he returned home, he talked extensively about his nonexistent war wounds, and sometimes even affected a limp. He even mysteriously claimed to have been awarded a Purple Heart medal, which is given to all soldiers wounded during wartime. No one knew that his only war-related injury actually resulted from a slip on a ship's ladder during a hazing ceremony. His campaign worked. He was elected, as a Republican, to the United States Senate in 1947.

Strangely, one of his first actions as a senator was to defend Nazi soldiers accused of gunning down American prisoners during the war. He did not mix with his fellow senators, and his roughshod manner did not make him any friends in Washington.

He discovered the political power of anti-Communism almost by accident. Addressing a friendly Republican group at a Lincoln Day dinner in Wheeling, West Virginia, in February 1950, McCarthy made a startling accusation about the presence of Communists in the United States government. "I have here in my hand," he roared, "a list of 205—a list of names that were made known to the Secretary of State as being members of the Communist Party and who nevertheless are still working and shaping policy in the State Department." McCarthy did not expect the reaction that developed. After all, he really had no names of proven Communists and the list he referred to was years old and already had been carefully investigated. Nonetheless, the senator became an overnight sensation.

Then, concerned about justifying his charge, he changed the number of alleged Communists from 205 to 57. Later, when he spoke in the Senate, the number became 81. He quickly discovered that regardless of the truth, charges against "card-carrying Communists" in government made newspaper headlines all over the country. He never had to prove anything. When one charge began to lose steam, he just moved on to another innocent victim and another reckless accusation. It was no matter to him that he left behind ruined careers and destroyed reputations. He never did find a single proven Communist in government.

In the early 1950s, Joe McCarthy was the best-known and most-feared member of the United States Senate. From his position as head of the Senate's Government Operations Committee and its Permanent Subcommittee on Investigations, he carried on a continual public and sensational circus. He did not invent anti-Communism, but quickly became its best-known spokesperson. Again and again he repeated his famous words, "I have here in my hand . . ." and went on to yet another unsubstantiated charge and the destruction of another innocent person's reputation. Accused people who invoked their rights under the Fifth Amendment of the United States Constitution were cleverly branded "Fifth-Amendment Communists" by McCarthy.

His accusations held Congress, governmental agencies, the academic world, and segments of the business world, notably the entertainment industry, in fear. Otherwise innocent individuals were dismissed from jobs, blacklists of suspected "disloyal" people were circulated widely, and an unwritten state of "self-censorship" enveloped the nation.

McCarthy tried to ban books from governmental libraries abroad that he claimed were written by Communists or "pinko" sympathizers. His list included some of America's best-known writers and most important literary works. Senators who opposed him lost reelection. Even President Dwight Eisenhower, a Republican who personally abhorred McCarthyism, refused to criticize the senator publicly. Privately, Eisenhower said, "I will not get into the gutter with that guy." Eisenhower expressed his personal outrage when he addressed the graduating class of Dartmouth College in 1953. "Don't join the book burners," he told the seniors. "Don't be afraid to go into your library and read every book!"

McCarthy's recklessness grew. He accused one of the country's two major political parties of treason. "Those who wear the label *Democrat*," he charged, "wear with it the stain of a historic betrayal. . . ." By early 1952, he turned his attention to alleged Communist infiltration of the United States Army. He demanded official army records, sent his staff on investigative trips, and made unproven charges. Then, in February 1954, he learned about a drafted army dentist at Camp Kilmer, Irving Peress, who had refused to answer questions on an army form about his political associations. The army was routinely investigating the situation when Peress, along with seven thousand other medical officers, was automatically advanced in rank strictly according to regulation. McCarthy was overjoyed. Here was a case he could use.

"Who promoted Peress?" he and his supporters cried. General Bernard Zwicker, a highly decorated World War II hero and the commander of Camp Kilmer, was summoned before McCarthy's committee and subjected to a savage and humiliating verbal attack. Cameras recorded every insult. People were shocked at the disrespectful way McCarthy questioned the military hero about the Peress case. At one point, the senator lectured Zwicker, "General, let's try and be truthful." Zwicker, angered nearly beyond words, responded, "I don't like to have anyone impugn my honesty, which you just did." McCarthy continued the verbal slugfest by adding, "Either your honesty or your intelligence!" The verbal bullying intensified. "General, you should be removed from any command. Any man who has been given the honor of being promoted to general and who says, 'I will protect another general who protected Communists,' is not fit to wear that uniform, General." McCarthy had escalated his recklessness into a full-scale war with the United States Army.

On the morning of March 9, as the *See It Now* staff in New York prepared for that night's program on Senator McCarthy, a courtly and respected politician rose to address his colleagues in the United States Senate. Vermont's Senator Ralph W. Flanders, a Republican, was upset at McCarthy's embarrassing antics. He accused the Wisconsin Senator of setting up "a one-man party—McCarthyism." Then, mocking McCarthy's inability to prove Communist infiltration of the army, Flanders continued: "He dons his war paint. He goes into his war dance. He emits his war whoops. He goes forth to battle and proudly returns with the scalp of a 'pink' army dentist. We may assume that this represents the depth and seriousness of Communist penetration at this time."

That evening, Edward R. Murrow opened his broadcast with a brief explanation and an invitation.

Because a report on Senator McCarthy is by definition controversial, we want to say exactly what we mean to say and I request your permission to read from the script whatever remarks Murrow and Friendly may make. If the Senator believes we have done violence to his words or pictures and desires to speak, to answer himself, an opportunity will be afforded him on this program.

Most of the program showed film clips of Senator McCarthy in action, bullying witnesses and making contradictory charges. Interjecting his own words only when necessary, Murrow skillfully provided a less than unbiased commentary.

On one thing the Senator has been consistent. Often operating as a one-man committee, he has traveled far, interviewed many, terrorized some, accused civilian and military leaders of the past administration of a great conspiracy to turn over the country to Communism, investigated and substantially demoralized the present State Department, made varying charges of espionage at Fort Monmouth.

Murrow quoted Senator Flanders' remarks of that morning and turned to a filmed speech McCarthy had given in Philadelphia on the Zwicker testimony. The clip showed McCarthy at his insulting best.

If a stupid, arrogant, or witless man in a position of power appears before our Committee and is found aiding the Communist Party, he will be exposed. The fact that he might be a general places him in no special class as far as I am concerned.

Then, looking directly into the camera, Murrow described McCarthy's typical methods. "Two of the staples of his diet are the investigations (protected by immunity) and the half truth." Using scenes from previous McCarthy speeches, Murrow presented examples of both methods in the senator's own words. Particularly revealing was the testimony before Senator McCarthy's subcommittee of Reed Harris, a longtime State Department employee who had just been dismissed from his position. The questioning focused on a book Harris had written in 1932 and the role of the American Civil Liberties Union (ACLU) in once providing him with an attorney's services. McCarthy's implication was that Harris must be guilty of something because his book contained unpopular material and the ACLU had once represented him. Murrow concluded:

Senator McCarthy succeeded only in proving that Reed Harris had once written a bad book which the American people had proved twenty-two years ago by not buying it, which is what they eventually do with all bad ideas. . . . The Reed Harris hearing demonstrates one of the senator's techniques. Twice he said the American Civil Liberties Union was listed as a subversive front. The Attorney General's list does not and has never listed the ACLU as subversive nor does the FBI or any other federal government agency. And the American Civil Liberties Union holds in its files letters of commendation from President Truman, President Eisenhower, and General MacArthur.

Murrow proceeded to place McCarthy and his actions in perspective:

We must not confuse dissent with disloyalty. We must remember always that accusation is not proof and that conviction depends upon evidence and due process of law. We will not walk in fear, one of another. We will not be driven by fear into an age of unreason if we dig deep in our history and our doctrine, and remember that we are not descended from fearful men, not from men who feared to write, to speak, to associate, and to defend causes that were for the moment unpopular.

Then came Murrow's final words—words that continue to remind succeeding generations of broadcast journalism's power to affect public opinion. As usual, Murrow spoke in his deep, well-modulated voice of authority, his face tightly framed by the television screen, his eyes seemingly riveted to each individual viewer.

This is no time for men who oppose Senator McCarthy's methods to keep silent, or for those who approve. We can deny our heritage and our history but we cannot escape responsibility for the result. . . . The actions of the junior senator from Wisconsin have caused alarm and dismay amongst our allies abroad and given considerable comfort to our enemies, and whose fault is that? Not really his, he didn't create this situation of fear, he merely exploited it and rather successfully. Cassius was right, "The fault, dear Brutus, is not in our stars, but in ourselves." Good night, and good luck.

The credits began to roll. The program was over. People in the control room, some with tears in their eyes, applauded.

Almost immediately, an outpouring of telegrams and phone calls descended upon CBS headquarters. A quick tally showed the reaction running overwhelmingly in favor of Murrow and against McCarthy. Many Americans were delighted to see McCarthy unmasked by his own words and threats. Helen Keller wrote Murrow, "Words cannot express my high admiration of the valiant attitude you have adopted in the present crisis of American history. I am with you heart and soul in your defiance of hostile elements that would impose the yoke of fear upon a free people."

Radio and television critic John Crosby, writing in the *New York Herald Tribune* on March 12, said, "The greatest witness against McCarthy was McCarthy himself. Sneering, truculent and wholly evil, he rumbled his evasions and hesitations and lies in a way that must have been a little shocking even to staunch McCarthyites. A couple of times he was caught huffing and chuckling in a way that sounded as if he were just a little nutty." Jack Gould wrote in the *New York Times*, "For TV, so often plagued by timidity and hesitation, the program was a milestone. . . ." *Broadcasting and Telecasting* magazine said, "They'll have to rewrite the definition of journalism now. No greater feat of journalistic enterprise has occurred in modern times than that performed by Ed Murrow last Tuesday."

Not all reaction to the *See It Now* program was favorable. The rabidly anti-Communist newsletter *The New Counterattack* devoted its March 19, 1954, issue to the question, "Why does the Communist press praise Edward R. Murrow so highly?" And in the *New York Journal American*, Jack O'Brian, a McCarthy supporter, wrote, "Murrow's techniques on radio and TV are identical. He stubbornly sticks to the left side of any situation. He states cases as fact when they are merely Murrow's opinion."

Appearing on Fulton Lewis Jr.'s news commentary program on the Mutual Broadcasting Network on March 11, McCarthy made charges of his own against Murrow. "I never listen to the extreme left-wing bleeding-heart elements of radio or television. However, after you invited me to come over here and appear on your program, I checked into Mr. Murrow's background a bit and you'll note I have in my hand a copy of the *Pittsburgh Sun-Telegram*." The senator then proceeded to describe a story about a summer-school program scheduled at Moscow State University in 1935. At the time, Edward R. Murrow was the assistant director of the American sponsoring organization. "This may explain," McCarthy continued, "why Edward R. Murrow, week after week, feels that he must smear McCarthy. . . . Maybe Mr. Murrow was worried about the exposure of some of his friends—I don't know."

McCarthy also told Fulton Lewis Jr. that Murrow was "not telling the truth" about the American Civil Liberties Union. Murrow later countered the charges and clearly stated, as he had on the March 9 broadcast, that the ACLU had never been on the attorney general's list of subversive organizations.

McCarthy accepted Murrow's invitation to appear on an upcoming *See It Now*. Not live, however. McCarthy hired an independent film studio to record his remarks with the assurance from Murrow that they would be broadcast in full. McCarthy told Murrow by telegram, "Normally I would not waste the time to merely prove that a radio and TV commentator who attacks me is lying. However, if I am correct in my position that you have consciously served the Communist cause, then it is very important for your listeners to have the clear-cut documented facts so they can decide whether or not you are as truthful as you attempt to make out or deliberately misrepresenting the facts."

In between the two McCarthy programs, *See It Now*, on March 16, broadcast another illuminating view of McCarthyism in action. McCarthy had brought a woman, Annie Lee Moss, before his committee on charges that she, a State Department employee with access to secret documents, was a member of the Communist Party. "Mrs. Moss," McCarthy began the questioning before the working cameras, "let me say for the record that you are not here because you are considered important in the Communist apparatus. We have the testimony that you are or have been a Communist."

As the questioning continued, it soon became clear to everyone present that the frightened, middle-aged woman seated primly before them hadn't the slightest idea why she was there. She didn't even know the meaning of the word *espionage*. One senator asked if she had ever talked to a Communist. Mrs. Moss answered, "No, sir—not to my knowledge." When he asked if she had ever heard of Karl Marx (the founder of Communism), she quickly replied, "Who's that?" The audience laughed. Indeed, it turned out that there were three other Annie Lee Mosses in the Washington telephone book. An obvious error had been made with the cameras recording every embarrassing moment. McCarthy quickly excused himself and left the chamber. In the program on the Moss hearing, Murrow did not comment on the woman's political affiliations but focused only on her right to face her accusers.

The McCarthy rebuttal aired on April 6, 1954. After a short introduction by Murrow, Senator Joseph McCarthy, on film, came out swinging. His very first sentence contained an error as he referred to Murrow as the "educational director of the Columbia Broadcasting System," a position last held by Murrow in 1936. It was clear to viewers that Joe McCarthy was no Ed Murrow. As in the film clips shown on the March 9 program, the senator had more the appearance of a street bully than a lawmaker. His voice was shrill and whiny; his language—sharp, blunt, and outrageous.

The half hour was vintage McCarthy, filled with innuendo, false accusations, and half-truths aimed at Ed Murrow, the senator's latest target. "Murrow is a symbol," the senator charged, "the leader and the cleverest of the jackal pack which is always found at the throat of anyone who dares to expose individual Communists and traitors." In a rambling, sometimes menacing discourse, which included a skewed history of world Communism, he managed to quote—out of context, as usual—statements from Communist publications which he conveniently connected with Murrow. He took special glee in the March 9 issue of the Communist Party's newspaper in which *See It Now* was referred to as "one of tonight's best bets on TV."

He lashed out wildly, twisting seemingly innocent events into great Communist conspiracies involving Murrow. Citing the dedication of a book to Murrow by English Socialist politician Harold Laski, McCarthy tried to make that innocent gesture of friendship appear sinister and unpatriotic. In true McCarthy style, unable to provide proof of his many charges, he told viewers, "Much of the documentation which we have here on the table tonight will not be available to the

American people by way of television. However, this will all be made available to you within the next two weeks." It never was.

Ed Murrow, not heard at all during the film, ended the program simply and calmly.

That was a film of Senator Joseph R. McCarthy, presented at our invitation. It was in response to a program we presented on March 9th. This reporter undertook to make no comment at this time, but naturally reserved his right to do so subsequently. Good night and good luck!

Murrow was prepared for the onslaught of charges. CBS officially released a statement supporting Murrow "as a broadcaster and as a loyal American." Murrow met with reporters and refuted each and every charge McCarthy had leveled against him. "Senator McCarthy's reckless and unfounded attempt to impugn my loyalty is just one more example of his typical tactic of attempting to tie up to Communism anyone who disagrees with him."

In turn, Murrow responded to each of McCarthy's charges. The summer school McCarthy claimed linked Murrow to the Soviet Union never was held. The newspaper story that mentioned the school did not prove any connection between Murrow and the Soviet government. As for the Laski book dedication, Murrow said, "Professor Laski was a British scholar and Socialist politician. He was a friend of mine. He is dead. He was a Socialist. I am not."

McCarthy's battle with the United States Army resumed on April 22, 1954. This time, the army was on the offensive. The Army-McCarthy Hearings were televised live. For weeks,

Americans saw McCarthy in action constantly interrupting witnesses and fellow senators with cries of "Point of order, Mr. Chairman, point of order!" As in previous appearances at televised hearings, he thrust himself constantly into the forefront with comments, charges, and questions. Even his formerly loyal supporters wearied of his boorish behavior and reckless disregard for truth.

When attorneys for the army proved that a photograph introduced in evidence by McCarthy had been "doctored" by the senator's aide, the public was treated to a humorous exchange. The army attorney, referring to the photo, asked a witness, "Did you think this came from a pixie?" McCarthy, in an attempt at humor, interrupted. "Will counsel for my benefit define—I think he might be an expert on that—what a pixie is?" The attorney quickly replied, "Yes, I should say, Mr. Senator, that a pixie is a close relative of a fairy. Shall I proceed, sir? Have I enlightened you?" The audience laughed. Senator McCarthy did not.

McCarthy and his methods were discredited before the entire nation. On December 2, 1954, Senator Joseph McCarthy of Wisconsin was officially censured—condemned—by the United States Senate. His power over America quickly diminished. He died two and a half years later a broken man. His death was attributed by many to his heavy reliance on alcohol. Others said it was television and Edward R. Murrow's incisive and daring reporting that really killed McCarthy.

*Little Egbert Roscoe Murrow, 1909 (WSU)*

# CHAPTER TWO

# From Polecat Creek to Pullman

*He couldn't wait to grow up.*
    —Ethel Murrow

"He didn't go canoeing to go canoeing, he went canoeing to go fishing. We walked in the woods and over the land—that was fun to do—but if you could do that and go hunting, too, that would be better." That's how Casey Murrow remembered his father's lifetime relationship with the outdoors, a relationship shaped early by the rigorous realities of life.

Egbert Roscoe Murrow—he became Edward later—was born on April 25, 1908, in a small log cabin in the woods at Polecat Creek, not far from Greensboro, North Carolina. He was the youngest of Ethel and Roscoe Murrow's three sons, and right from birth, seemed the loudest. His older brothers teased him and called him "Egg" and "Eber Blowhard." The Murrows lived on a small farm and worked hard to eke out a living growing cotton, watermelons, and tobacco. Often, the only sight the boys had of their father was of him plowing the land behind a mule team from sunrise to sunset. The boys worked hard, too. When Egbert grew old enough to carry a pail, he began feeding the chickens and slopping the pigs.

Ethel and Roscoe Murrow were a loving couple but completely opposite in appearance and disposition. Roscoe, a hulking six-footer, had an easy manner and cheery attitude. Ethel, in contrast, was a tiny, religious woman who ruled her household, and all in it, in a firm, unbending manner. Janet Murrow, Edward's wife, later recounted that Ethel "was a definite personality, I couldn't imagine doing anything wrong [around] her." Ethel always worried. Even when there was nothing to worry about, she worried. If the boys were late coming home for dinner, she imagined them lying dead in the woods. While she was not outwardly affectionate toward the boys, she loved them dearly. Her goal was to assure that her sons succeed and live their lives with honor and faith.

The Murrows were part of a close-knit larger community of relatives and friends who lived nearby. No electricity reached the Murrow farm. Young Egbert's earliest memories were of hunting, playing in the outdoors, eating watermelon, and listening to intricate Civil War stories told by his grandfather, George Van Buren Lamb, known by all as Captain Van, an authentic Confederate Army war hero. Ethel, the captain's daughter, inherited her father's art of storytelling. Her children, Egbert, Dewey, and Lacey, grew up to stories of battles, country life, and the Bible. Edward R. Murrow later credited those early storytelling experiences for his lifelong interest in history.

The Murrow attachment to the land went back many generations. But Roscoe Murrow wanted a better life for his family. The uncertain life of a poor farmer, even if he did own the land, did not offer him the security he wanted. He was also concerned about Ethel, who suffered from asthma. When their relatives, the Cobles, left North Carolina to settle in far-off Washington State, Roscoe was more than keenly interested in their journey. In 1914, when Egbert was six years old, Roscoe decided that it was in the family's best economic and health interests to follow the Cobles west to a new life.

The train trip across the country took six days. Ethel, partly to save money and partly to avoid the unknown germs of trackside restaurants along the way, packed two huge wicker baskets with food, mainly fried chicken. The only food the boys could buy during the trip was fresh fruit from station vendors.

Their long trip ended in Blanchard, Washington, a town of wooden sidewalks and muddy streets in the heart of timber country. Until Roscoe could find work, the family set up housekeeping in a tent on the property of their Coble cousins. Finding work was not easy. At first, Roscoe hired himself out as a farmhand, but it was not easy for the former landowner to work as a hired hand on other people's farms. The future did not look any more promising here than it had in Polecat Creek. Indeed, within a few months, the family journeyed back to North Carolina partly to visit and partly to make certain they had made the right decision by leaving their ancestral land. The visit over, they returned to their new home with hope of a better future.

Life improved upon their return to Washington. Roscoe found a job with a local logging company and the family moved from the tent to a sturdy wooden house in town. Within a short time, Roscoe was transferred as a brakeman on the logging company's railroad. Ethel was very strict and quite demanding of her boys. She expected them to behave properly and she did not condone idleness. The boys went to school and worked odd jobs in their spare time. Egbert later remarked that although he lived near water, he never learned to swim "because there was always work to do." During the summers, the brothers mowed lawns, weeded beets, and hoed corn.

Ethel became active in church and community life and was soon elected treasurer of the local school board. She was always concerned about her boys' well-being. One neighbor recalled that at afternoon community meetings, Ethel's reports came early, "for when it was time for the children to come home from school, there was no holding her." As devoted a mother as Ethel was, she also had a strong sense of community responsibility, which sometimes overtook family concerns. When her oldest son, Lacey, graduated from college, she canceled her trip to the ceremony when she learned that a neighbor had been gravely injured in an accident. She sent a quick telegram to her son informing him that she could not come because she had to attend to the injured man and his family. Lacey was so devastated, he ignored the graduation and left immediately for an awaiting job.

The Blanchard Grade School, which the three boys attended, was no more than a two-room building. Egbert began his studies there in 1914 when he was six years old and remained there until he turned fourteen. His favorite subjects were English, history, and geography. Throughout his life, he never did well with arithmetic or spelling. But he did like to debate, about everything. He was hot-tempered and never at a loss for words. At home, he took the opposite side of any question.

He maintained a running battle of wits with an equally stubborn neighbor, a Mr. Bickel, who in exasperation told Mrs. Murrow, "You'd better watch that boy! He's either going to be a great man or a very bad man!" Ethel then worried whether Egbert would grow up only to be hanged as a criminal!

The warm family relationship was anchored in the firm religious faith Ethel brought with her from North Carolina. The boys attended Sunday school regularly. Mrs. Murrow later recounted, "I read a chapter from the Bible aloud to them every night of their lives before they went to bed, until we had read through the entire book." Years later, in a letter to his mother, Edward R. Murrow wrote the following:

The more I see of the world's great, the more convinced I am that you gave us the basic equipment—something that is as good in a palace as in a foxhole. Love, respect, cooperation, discipline, and religious instruction—could any child psychologist, after years of study, give us better advice for rearing children than that?

The boys' relationship with their father was more informal. His sons liked to be with him. Roscoe taught them to shoot and hunt and respect the outdoors. Although the family was not poverty-stricken, money was always a consideration. Egbert became a good shot because, as he later recalled, "shells cost money." The male Murrows enjoyed working and playing together. Roscoe was a large man who appeared tough, yet was a gentle, caring person. As befitted someone who worked amid giant trees and huge, steam-belching locomotives, he was often rough with equipment and machinery. He and the boys worked on the family cars together. A family story recalls the time they rebuilt the engine of a used car. When they started it up, the engine's piston rod blew straight through the garage roof!

Each boy, in turn, attended high school in Edison, five miles away, since their own town was too small to have its own high school. In 1922, Lacey became the first of the Murrow boys to enroll at Washington State University. Just like his older brothers when they turned fourteen, Egbert followed their lead into permanent school-vacation jobs with the lumber company that employed their father. That first summer in the logging camps, Egbert worked as a "whistle punk" precariously riding on top of a logging train. His job was to signal the crews. It was not a difficult job, but it was dangerous.

Egbert approached high school with the same zeal as his brothers before him. Like them, he participated in a wide variety of school activities. He played basketball in winter and baseball in spring, sang in the glee club, and acted in school musical plays. In his senior year, in 1925, he was elected class president and graduated first in his class. He was named the boy who had done most for the school. Dewey had graduated from Edison two years earlier and had been captain of the debate team. Egbert was invited to join and continue the family tradition. Normally at no loss for words, the younger brother was nervous and felt out of place in the formal debate setting. His English teacher, who was also the debate team coach, encouraged him. Young Egbert went on to lead the team to a regional championship. Under his yearbook picture was a quotation from Shakespeare: "A man in the world's new fashion planted/that hath a mint of phrases in his brain."

During his last two years at Edison High, Egbert succeeded

his brother, Dewey, as driver of the school's makeshift Model T bus. The circuit of the thirty-mile round trip took about two hours to complete each way. The route included eight unguarded train crossings and rough terrain. Ethel worried constantly. "Those were the worst two years of my life!" she later said. "I thought I was done for then," she added, "for Ed was not as careful and deliberate as Dewey and I didn't know a minute's peace, especially on those terrible, foggy days."

The year 1925 also saw an abrupt change for the entire Murrow family. The usually mild-mannered Roscoe was being harassed at work by a supervisor. Finally, unwilling to suffer the abuse any longer, he punched the man in the jaw and quit his job. Luckily, he soon found a job with another timber company one hundred miles west in remote Beaver, Washington, in the Olympic Rain Forest. The move meant the uprooting of the home and community ties established in Blanchard over twelve years. They had no choice.

Egbert held a secret hope of attending the University of Virginia to study law. Given the family's economic condition, this was not a realistic goal. To earn money for college, the young man, who had spent his high-school vacations working in the forests, decided to take a year off before college and go to work for his father's new employer. Egbert's first job for the Bloedell-Donovan Company was as an ax man. He was part of a team that went out into the forests to fell trees. The work was hard and unyielding but Egbert, now grown to over six feet in height, relished the challenge of the outdoors. Years later, when he was already a famous broadcaster, he modestly said, "Even now, I'm probably more proficient with an ax than I am with a typewriter." In fact, during the filming of a news show in the 1950s, about logging, he requested permission from a surprised foreman to use the signal whistle. His days as a whistle punk replayed in his mind as he, incautiously, signaled the rapid relay of a heavy log down the mountain.

Within a short time, he was made assistant to a timber cruiser, the person responsible for marking out areas of virgin forest for cutting. He loved that job and the courageous outdoor lives of the lumberjacks. For weeks at a time, he and the timber cruiser set out alone into uncharted forests to survey and map the next section for harvesting. They usually camped out by themselves under the stars. On the occasions when they went into one of the isolated lumber camps, they joined the loggers around the campfire to swap stories and sing lively logging songs. In the process, Egbert, the most popular member of his high-school class, was transformed into Ed, the handsome, well-liked logger who, to his mother's chagrin, was now also a confirmed drinker and smoker. During that year of adventure, he gained not only an in-depth view of the timber industry but a rich vocabulary of profanity. He later remarked, "This is a fabulous country and to this day offers exciting pictorial possibilities."

The money he earned during that year was far from enough to pay his way to the University of Virginia. Ed Murrow gave up on that dream, and followed his brothers to Washington State University in Pullman. For the young man who had spent the previous year in the woods in the fellowship of rough-and-tumble men, the first days on campus were a shock. The neat lawns and symmetrical red-brick buildings contrasted sharply with the majestic outdoor cathedral of ice-capped mountains and endless carpet of green forests. But wherever he went, he always remembered his roots. At the end of his life, he wrote to his brother, "I have never forgotten where I came from. The land was a part of one, the people were in my heart, and it all defined my vision for a long time to come."

*Murrow (far right) with other WSU students (WSU)*

# CHAPTER THREE

# The Student Prince

*He was so confident and mature.*
        —Justice Lewis Powell

In 1926, Pullman, Washington, was a small town of fewer than thirty thousand people. With no industrial or manufacturing base, its only business was the state college on the hill which annually attracted three thousand undergraduate students to its distinctive campus. For Ed Murrow, Washington State University was not just a "cow college," it was a totally new world.

While the experiences were new, the old concern with money remained. Before even registering for his first college class, Ed went in search of work. The money earned during his year in the logging camps could only go so far. To his good fortune, he quickly found work in a college sorority house as part-time janitor and dishwasher. The job provided him with a small but comfortable room in the basement, which he shared with another boy, Ed Lehan. On weekends, he often worked in the Pullman railroad yards loading heavy grain sacks. Living in the sorority house was pleasant enough and provided him with an added benefit. Lying in his basement room, he and his roommate could overhear the sorority sisters on the floor above sharing secrets. "Very informative," Murrow later quipped.

He had graduated at the top of his small high-school class, but he was not ready for the academic decisions that faced him at college. With no specific career in mind, he decided to major in business. Following in his brothers' footsteps, he became an active member of the Reserve Officer Training Corps (ROTC), the U.S. Army's college program for future reserve officers. Lacey had graduated as the ROTC cadet colonel, the highest student rank. Ed enjoyed the marching, drilling, and camaraderie. He especially liked the uniform. The highest grade he earned the first semester was an A in ROTC.

Student life on campus revolved around the activities of sororities and fraternities. Ed was accepted into Kappa Sigma, considered the most prestigious fraternity on campus. Kappa Sigma was yet another legacy of his older brothers. Although there was little time left for studying, Ed's busy extracurricular activities did not seem to affect his grades adversely. His roommate once said, "He had a photographic mind. He could sit through classes all week and never take a note, but on Friday nights, he could rattle off the professors' lectures almost verbatim."

Although not living in the fraternity house was a disadvantage, Ed spent much time with his Kappa Sigma brothers on weekends. They were greatly impressed by young Murrow's ability to consume vast amounts of liquor with no signs of drunkenness. He intrigued them with stories of life in the forests, experiences the other boys could only envy. Slightly awestruck, they gave him his fraternity nickname, "Tall Timber."

When it came time to choose classes for second semester,

Ed heard about a wonderful speech course his roommate was taking. Remembering his own successful high-school debating experiences, Ed went to see the teacher. That meeting changed Edward R. Murrow's life.

Herself a recent graduate of Washington State, the teacher was not much older than her students. Ida Lou Anderson did not make an imposing first impression. She was, as a student described her, "cruelly dwarfed, hunched and twisted." But the polio that had so deformed her body had not in any way diminished her intelligence or her magnificent gift of speech.

Ida Lou Anderson was an unusual teacher. Her keen thinking abilities, distinct accuracy in speech, knowledge of literature, and love of poetry drew attention away from her striking physical deformity. Recalling her impact on students, the Washington State president said, "She was genuinely interested in them and . . . helped them to see themselves objectively and to realize their full capacities."

The mutual attraction between the cultured teacher and the boy from the backwoods was not instantaneous. Ed had to use all his persuasiveness and charm to gain admission to her class. Once there, he quickly demonstrated the appropriateness of the move. Another student later said, "She was Ed Murrow's favorite teacher. He was Ida Lou's favorite student." For the rest of his four years at Washington State, Ed Murrow took every course Ida Lou Anderson taught.

Her philosophy of life and of teaching was expressed centuries earlier in her favorite selection from *The Meditations of Marcus Aurelius*—words Ed Murrow embraced for himself:

If thou workest at that which is before thee, following right reason seriously, vigorously, calmly, without allowing anything else to distract thee . . . but satisfied with thy present activity according to nature, and with heroic truth in every word and sound which thou utterest, thou wilt live happy.

Ida Lou Anderson saw great potential in the young man from the logging camps and took upon herself the task of properly educating him to his fullest potential. She invited Ed to visit her at home. There, she introduced him to the works of poets and writers she admired. As they talked about the extra assigned readings, Ed's intellectual curiosity was awakened.

At the same time, she drilled into him all the skills he would need to become a confident and effective speaker. She taught him to use pauses and intonations to best advantage and to use as few words as possible to make a point. He was an eager and talented student. In four years, Ed Murrow, who since boyhood had been a natural debater, was transformed into a polished professional by Ida Lou Anderson. "She demanded not excellence so much as integrity," Murrow later said.

As an upperclassman, Ed often accompanied Ida Lou to campus cultural events and dances. Years later, when Ed Murrow was a famous newscaster, Ida Lou Anderson listened proudly to his broadcasts but did not hesitate to send him suggestions for further improvement.

At the end of each school year, Ed returned home for the summer and a job that was always waiting for him at the lumber company. With the passing of time, he grew more sophisticated and the world in which he grew up took on a different look.

Ed entered his second year on campus with the confidence to enter mainstream student life actively. With financial support from his older brother, Lacey, Ed moved into his fraternity house. He continued to view each new campus experience as a learning opportunity by which to broaden his own limited view of the world. His circle of friends increased as did his popularity. He had transformed himself into a polished gentleman. Of his fraternity brothers he once said, perhaps with not a little exaggeration, "They taught me table manners."

Handsome and well spoken, Ed became a popular participant in a wide variety of campus affairs. During the second semester of his sophomore year, he was invited to join a secret, unofficial "super fraternity" of campus leaders. This small group operated like a big-city political machine and controlled nearly all aspects of campus political life. Ed was overwhelmingly elected president of the junior class. He showed an interest in drama and performed in campus plays. His grades suffered only slightly as he transformed his energies from the unseen labor of the earlier odd jobs to the unpaid glory of campus activism.

During the summer of 1928, the young man who had experienced more of life than any of his new friends, almost died. Working again for the logging company, he was caught in a raging forest fire and only escaped a horrible death by jumping into a stream. He survived without any visible injury, but the hot smoke he inhaled did not do his lungs any good.

On his return to school, Ed added courses in psychology, history, and sociology to his speech and ROTC classes. He got A's in his military and speech courses, but B's and C's in most of the others, including a C in physical education. His involvement in campus activities turned him into an expert in the fine art of political strategy. He enjoyed the intrigues and challenges. He dressed fashionably, cultivated an air of sophistication, and treated everyone, fellow students and professors, courteously. Girls were attracted to him; boys admired him. His senior yearbook described him as having "an A-plus personality, together with a level head."

He represented his school in debate competitions at other colleges and was elected president of the entire student body at Washington State during his senior year. He went to the annual convention of the Pacific Student Federation and was elected president of that regional organization of campus leaders. He returned to begin his senior year as appointed cadet colonel of ROTC, the highest rank a student could hold; the same rank held by his brother, Lacey, a few years earlier.

The National Student Federation of America (NSFA) was founded in 1925. Its members came from the student leadership of the country's most prestigious universities. Its aims, as described in its constitution, were to "achieve a spirit of cooperation among the students of the United States of America . . . [and to] foster understanding among the students of the world in the furtherance of an enduring peace." The NSFA's 1930 convention was scheduled for Stanford University in Palo Alto, California, in January.

Ed Murrow attended as president of the host region. It was an enlightening experience for the young man from Washington. He met and spoke with student leaders from all over the country representing differing opinions and views. The meetings were not one-sided. NSFA leaders, including Chester Williams from the University of California at Los Angeles and Lewis Powell from Virginia's Washington and Lee University, were looking for an imposing personality to take charge and represent the best interests of America's students. They quickly were convinced that Ed would be the ideal candidate for NSFA president.

Ed did not know how desperately NSFA was searching for the right leader when, as host president, he delivered a keynote speech to the entire convention. In a hard-hitting, well-delivered speech that Ida Lou Anderson would have applauded, Ed called upon his fellow students to face the challenges of the real world and see beyond the "fraternities, football, and fun" usually associated with college life. The delegates were greatly impressed.

Ed Murrow proudly returned to Pullman, Washington, as president of the National Student Federation of America. The Washington State school newspaper triumphed his return with the banner headline, ED MURROW IS ELECTED TO REPRESENT NATION.

During his final semester, he took a course on radio. The future broadcaster earned only a B. He graduated in June 1930, with the requirements for Phi Beta Kappa, the prestigious national honor society. However, he was not elected "because of a thundering row with a faculty member on the selection committee." The decorative key, presented to all members, would not be his until years later when he was given honorary membership.

When he entered college in 1926, it was with enthusiastic near-certainty that upon graduation the world would be open to him. No one anticipated the stock-market crash of 1929. By graduation day, the country had begun its slide into the Great Depression and jobs were scarce, even for energetic college graduates. His classmates, many of whom had never left Washington State, must have been envious when it was announced that Ed Murrow would travel extensively during that summer representing the NSFA.

At the conclusion of his trip, Ed was scheduled to direct the affairs of NSFA from its national headquarters in New York.

Instead of a salary, the organization settled upon the amount of twenty-five dollars per week to cover expenses. With no real job in sight, and the lure of travel and the excitement of New York, Edward R. Murrow gratefully accepted the opportunity. After visiting a number of NSFA regional offices, Ed arrived in New York toward the end of June 1930, with two suitcases and forty dollars.

The NSFA national headquarters was a crowded basement room in a rundown brick apartment building on Madison Avenue. Before he could settle in, he was on his way to Europe leading NSFA delegates to an international student congress in Belgium. His cabin mate on board the ship was a young man he had met at Palo Alto, Lewis Powell of Virginia. Powell planned to become a lawyer and Ed began referring to him as "judge." Years later, Powell was appointed a justice of the United States Supreme Court.

When the congress ended, Ed traveled through Europe. He met with student leaders and received an enlightening introduction to different cultures. His circle of contacts expanded to include men and women he would encounter again. He took special note of economic and political changes and returned to the United States a more worldly person.

Back in New York, he needed a place to live. Chester Williams, his friend from West Coast NSFA activities, had also come to New York to work at NSFA, so both newcomers decided to share a dingy walkup apartment on East Thirty-seventh Street. It was so cramped, they cooked on a hot plate in the bathroom. As poor as they were, they conceived a brilliant idea that allowed them to frequently dine well, attend the opera, or visit a nightclub.

The NSFA did not have funds to hire employees, but the

rich fathers of young women volunteers did. The women, recently graduated from America's finest colleges, were unable to find real jobs because of the Depression. With time on their hands, they volunteered at NSFA. They were wonderful workers, but volunteers are sometimes not as reliable as paid workers. Murrow and Williams approached the women's fathers, who were delighted to provide NSFA with funds which would be partially used to pay their daughters secretly. The women, meanwhile, did useful work and gained valuable experience. Indeed, when office finances hit rock bottom, these dedicated women even approached their willing parents for contributions to aid the cause.

NSFA activities were diverse, ranging from low-cost student trips to Europe to hosting foreign student debaters in the United States. As well, NSFA represented American students at important international student conferences.

In a public relations coup, Chester Williams worked out an arrangement with the Columbia Broadcasting System to produce a monthly radio program called *University of the Air*. CBS was anxious to fill surplus airtime with quality programming and thought NSFA could provide talks by famous personalities in politics and the arts. Williams and Murrow drew upon their ever-growing circle of acquaintances on both sides of the Atlantic to provide world-famous guests, ranging from the British prime minister to Albert Einstein. Working on the program gave Ed a practical education about radio broadcasting. His on-air debut took place in September 1930, when he hosted one of the programs.

In his travels to hundreds of college campuses, Ed observed that nearly all the NSFA members were white. Massive discrimination against African Americans was common, especially in the South. Ed decided that NSFA, representing all college students, had to set an example by integrating itself. He began visiting black colleges and enrolled a small number of African-American members. That was a start, but something dramatic was needed.

As it happened, the next NSFA convention was scheduled for Atlanta, Georgia, a still-segregated city. Not taking anything for granted, he planned every detail of the complicated maneuvering to integrate the Atlanta convention at the Biltmore Hotel. Murrow not only had to convince his own membership but also defuse possible legal problems with the hotel. The last part was easy. Murrow drew up a detailed addition to the standard hotel contract in which he listed the colleges to be represented at the convention. Included were the names of the all-black colleges. Luckily, the hotel management did not bother reading all the fine print and signed the contract, automatically obligating them to serve all delegates.

The first part was trickier. Murrow utilized all the political strategies he had learned in campus politics to skillfully control the heated board debates. To insure success at the general meetings, he took several unusual steps. He organized "flying squads" of liberal young women from exclusive colleges to calmly reassure anyone who might disrupt the proceedings. He also went to see Adolph Ochs, the venerable publisher of the *New York Times*. Murrow asked Ochs to assign a reporter to cover the convention in Atlanta. The NSFA meeting was not the type of event usually reported by the *Times*. But after hearing out the young man's reasons, Ochs understood the hidden motive and agreed to send a reporter to Atlanta.

At the opening meeting, white and black delegates were seated together. One white delegate took one look around, jumped from his seat, and headed for the door. A "flying squad" encircled him and asked him to reconsider. Their delaying tactic provided time for the *New York Times* reporter, a young man from Alabama, to approach. "Do you really want to walk out of this convention and force me to write a story that will make your college and all us Southerners appear to be bigots in the pages of that Yankee newspaper I work for?" the reporter asked softly in his best southern drawl. The young man sheepishly returned to his seat. Murrow had won a victory for racial integration.

There was one final battle to be fought in Atlanta—the closing banquet. The hotel simply would not serve African Americans. Murrow thought of a compromise. He seated black delegates with members of the versatile all-white "flying squad." The black waiters served the white women, who then passed the plates to the black delegates, before receiving second plates for themselves. The color barrier was broken.

At the final session of the convention, the delegates voted "not to discriminate against any applicant for membership because of race or color." The *New York Times* reported positively on the convention's activities and Ed Murrow was unanimously reelected president for a second term.

During the summer of 1931, Murrow returned to Europe. After attending an international student convention in Bucharest, Romania, he and two traveling companions spent several months touring Europe. The two trips to Europe were eye-opening experiences for the young man who had spent most of his life in rural America. As early as 1931, he could glimpse hints of the political and military changes about to overtake Europe. Everywhere he traveled he continued to meet student leaders and engage in lively political discussions.

He was gaining a first-rate education in diplomacy and foreign affairs, but still did not have a real job.

Aside from his travels, the two years at NSFA provided
solid learning experiences and opportunities to demonstrate
his many skills. His twenty-five-dollar-a-week expense check
was also welcome as the Great Depression worsened. He
wanted to work in higher education and gave some thought
to enrolling in a special program at Columbia University's
Teachers College to prepare for a position as a college admin-
istrator.

Then, in 1932, two job offers appeared almost simultaneously. The first came from Dr. Stephen Pierce Duggan,
founder and director of the Institute of International
Education (IIE). Duggan had observed Murrow's work at
NSFA and wanted the young man as his assistant director.
The IIE was founded in 1919 to promote better relations
between the United States and other countries. Murrow
described it as "a sort of unofficial educational embassy,
bringing foreign students to this country on fellowships, send-
ing Americans abroad, arranging exchange professorships,
publishing monographs."

The second job offer came from officials at the lumber
company that had employed him back in Washington. They
invited him to become the company's agent in Shanghai,
China, at a hefty yearly salary. Murrow, who fondly remembered the time spent in the timber camps, nonetheless accepted Dr. Duggan's lesser financial offer. He added two years to
his age on the job application to appear older for the high-pro-
file position.

Murrow resigned from the National Student Federation of
America and was elected an honorary board member as a

reward for his successful work. In many ways, his work at the IIE resembled what he did at NSFA. There were endless reports to write and proposals to evaluate. The IIE was a major sponsor of visiting foreign students in the United States, and he supervised the exchange students and arranged for their scholarships and travel. He still traveled extensively, but now he could afford to stay in decent hotels. Dr. Duggan was well known and Ed soon found himself in the company of the rich and famous as he attended to IIE business. Murrow also continued to arrange radio broadcasts.

Duggan was interested in improving contacts with educators in the Soviet Union at a time when the Soviets were viewed suspiciously by many Americans. He sincerely believed that world peace could be achieved through education, and encouraged his young assistant to plan summer educational programs in Moscow.

Murrow did not lose touch with the NSFA and, in December 1932, headed South for the annual convention. After a several-day stopover with relatives in Polecat Creek, North Carolina, he boarded a train to continue the trip to New Orleans. On board were other NSFA members and Ed greeted them warmly. He paid particular attention to one young woman, Janet Huntington Brewster, the student-body president from Mount Holyoke College in Massachusetts. When the convention ended, that attention had turned to romance, and Ed became a frequent visitor to the Mount Holyoke campus.

*Murrow in London, 1940 (WSU)*

## CHAPTER FOUR

# A Fateful Phone Call

*How would you like to go to Europe?*
　　　　　　　　—Ed Klauber

In the early 1930s, when radio was primarily a source of entertainment and curiosity, newspapers were the prime source of news. By mid-decade, one of the nation's top radio networks, the Columbia Broadcasting System (CBS), offered only three national news programs daily—one five-minute program at noon and one at 4:30 P.M. and a fifteen-minute program at 11:00 P.M. Not everyone realized the obvious power of radio to inform and influence people.

Two widely separated world leaders of the time well understood radio's potential power to influence public opinion. Franklin Delano Roosevelt, who inherited the ills of the Great Depression when he became president of the United States, used radio to assure Americans that "we have nothing to fear but fear itself." Across the Atlantic, the new ruler of

Germany, Adolph Hitler, used radio just as effectively to instill fear.

Through the tyrannical rule of his Nazi party, Hitler sought to eliminate any dissent to his views. Foremost among those Hitler perceived as enemies were the Jews. "The Jews are our misfortune" was a popular Nazi slogan of the time. Beginning in 1933, anti-Semitism—hatred of Jewish people— was the cornerstone of Nazi philosophy. Soon, political opponents, writers, teachers—anyone who opposed Hitler, Jewish and non-Jewish—began to disappear in Germany. Many were sent to prison, some died mysteriously. Others tried to flee.

Activities in Germany soon impacted upon the work of the IIE in New York. The office was flooded by frantic calls and letters from German professors desperately seeking positions at American universities. Deeply concerned, Stephen Duggan and others, late in 1933, formed the Committee in Aid of Displaced German Scholars. In charge of the day-to-day operations was Edward R. Murrow who, in addition to his regular IIE duties, was named secretary of the committee. "I was the youngster who did the donkey work," he later recalled.

For two years, Murrow personally handled all the correspondence and financial activities of the committee. With the help of aid from such organizations as the Rockefeller Foundation and the American Jewish Joint Distribution Committee, he raised over a million and a half dollars for the cause. He met and befriended dozens of the most respected scholars of the time, including Nobel Prize scientists and award-winning writers. All in all, he succeeded in placing three hundred of the world's most respected intellectuals in positions at leading American universities. But along the way, he had to combat resistance among American educators who, during the economic depression, feared the loss of their own jobs.

The importance of the work he did for the committee was not lost on Murrow. In his written report at the end of the first year, he compared the intellectual migration of the world's leading thinkers from Germany to the expulsion of the Jews from Spain in 1492. His committee work also personally affected him. "The best education I ever received came from German professors who were flung out of German universities by Hitler," he said. Reflecting further, he added, "It was the most personally satisfying undertaking in which I have ever engaged and contributed more to my knowledge of politics and international relations than any similar period in my life."

In keeping with Stephen Duggan's international outlook, the IIE continued to support visits by German exchange students to America even when the guests publicly espoused Nazi beliefs at their host universities. Those exchanges ended only with the outbreak of World War II in 1939.

Ed visited Janet whenever he could and maintained their ongoing courtship by mail. Janet was busy, too. She had majored in economics and sociology and originally foresaw a career for herself working for a department store or perhaps as a social worker. But after graduation from Mount Holyoke, she accepted a position at her hometown high school, where she taught English and commercial law.

Janet and Ed were married on October 27, 1934, at the Brewster home in Middletown, Connecticut. It was a small

gathering and no one from the Murrow family was in attendance. The newlyweds set out on a two-month honeymoon
trip by automobile. The nearly exhausted bridegroom had
earned his vacation. They traveled to North Carolina to visit
relatives and then to Washington to visit Ed's parents. Ed
enjoyed showing Janet the sights of his childhood. They even
took a trip to Pullman so Janet could meet Ida Lou Anderson.

The trip was not all pleasure. Although he was technically
on a leave of absence, Ed visited universities to address student and faculty groups. He was in constant contact with IIE
headquarters and sent Dr. Duggan frequent reports on the
mood of American educators concerning the influx of foreign
professors. When he arrived at his parents' home, a thick
package of correspondence and reports from New York
awaited him.

On their return to New York, the couple settled into a comfortable apartment on the East Side. Janet immediately joined
the social whirl of IIE activities. They were invited to the
homes of well-known IIE supporters. In turn, Janet arranged
for dinner parties at the Murrow apartment. In recognition of
his hard work, Ed was appointed a member of the prestigious
Council on Foreign Relations.

In 1934, Dr. Duggan began broadcasting over CBS on the
*American School of the Air,* a program about educational issues.
Ed was assigned the task of lining up guest speakers and
attending to the relations between IIE and CBS. From time to
time, Ed was the on-air host for programs. He became
acquainted with Fred Willis, newly appointed director of education for the network. Ed was already familiar with the inner
workings of radio from his experience at NSFA. The follow-

ing year, when CBS wanted to expand its educational programming, Willis thought of Ed Murrow.

As dedicated as Murrow was to Dr. Duggan and the institute, the young man began to realize that advancement within IIE was limited. Duggan had no plans to retire or share
leadership with anyone else. Murrow, at age twenty-seven and
recently married, decided it was time to make a career
change. Willis invited Ed to interview for a newly created
position at CBS, "director of talks." In reality, the job would
be very similar to what he had been doing first for NSFA and
now for IIE. He would be responsible for tracking down and
hiring suitable guest speakers for a variety of network programs dealing with education and current affairs. The job was
strictly administrative; he would not be an on-air personality.

Ed did not instantly pursue the CBS job offer. In June 1935,
Ed and Janet traveled to Europe on IIE business. The institute
only paid for Ed's expenses, so the young couple worked their
way across the Atlantic as social directors on the Dutch liner
*Statendam*. For most of the voyage, while Ed organized volley-
ball and bingo for the guests, Janet lay suffering from seasick-
ness in their small cabin.

This was Janet's first trip to Europe and Ed, already a seasoned traveler, was her tour guide. They visited England,
France, and Germany and met previous IIE contacts while
expanding the Murrow list of European friends. In England,
with the CBS job offer in mind, Ed met with Cesar
Saerchinger, CBS's European representative. In Germany,
Nazi decrees spread fear among academics. Janet wondered at
the large number of hushed telephone calls and secret visitors

to their hotel room as Jewish and non-Jewish professors appealed to Ed for help.

On their return to New York in early September, the CBS job offer weighed heavily on their minds. It was difficult for Ed to leave IIE, but he needed to move on. "We thought we'd spend the rest of our lives in education," Janet Murrow said. "Ed had quite a debate . . . about whether to leave the foundation world. . . ." Finally, he accepted the position as director of talks for CBS in charge of all political, educational, and religious broadcasts.

Ed left the IIE with solid experience which he would now apply to broadcasting. In a 1932 letter to his mother, Ed clearly defined his reporting philosophy.

I learned how one can negate the seriousness of a human problem by putting it in terms of statistics. . . . I found that I could get my point across with more power if only I learned how to reduce a problem to its most basic essence—namely, how one human being suffered at the hands of political repression. . . . By reducing a problem in this way, it is much easier to feel the way a real person feels. This, I think, is a good thing to learn.

When the Federal Communications Commission was established in 1927 to regulate the growing broadcasting business, it set down a requirement that radio networks provide "some sort of news or public affairs" programming. CBS established a small department to arrange "educational talks." Ed's only guidance from his superiors was to avoid "subjects or personalities of a controversial nature."

He quickly set to work arranging broadcasts by noted political figures. That part of the job did not differ much from what he had done at the IIE, but with one major difference. He became the buffer between the network and disgruntled politicians upset by the assignment of broadcast times. "This job," as later described in *Scribner's* magazine, "dusted off any remaining academic cobwebs on Murrow and prepared him for international radio."

On Christmas Eve 1936, the CBS office party and related drinking sputtered to an end as the evening news broadcast was about to begin. The network's staff announcer, a young man by the name of Robert Trout, was at his usual place in front of the microphone. As he was about to open the broadcast, Ed Murrow playfully yanked the script away and began reading the news into the microphone. There was nothing Trout could do but stand by. It was Ed Murrow's first—but highly irregular—news broadcast for CBS.

Murrow enjoyed his new responsibilities. His work was much appreciated at the network. CBS President William Paley began to take notice of the young director of talks and the two began a personal and professional friendship that lasted for decades. When the position of European director became vacant, Paley wanted Murrow for the job.


When I first met him, I was so impressed . . . he was such a sober, earnest young man at twenty-seven, with that elongated, somber face—that I wrote a memo to Ed Klauber, who had hired him: "Mr. Murrow might be the best one in this organization to be responsible for all our international broadcasting."

Part of Murrow's network responsibilities extended to coverage of educational matters. His previous associations with the NSFA and the IIE had left him with innumerable contacts in the educational field. He was a frequent attendee at educational gatherings where he arranged for network broadcasts. In February 1937, Ed and Janet were in New Orleans attending the annual convention of the National Education Association. When the phone rang in their hotel room, Ed answered. On the line was his boss, Ed Klauber, a CBS vice president. "How would you like to go to Europe?" Murrow, by now an experienced traveler, answered, "Fine, I always like to go to Europe, but what do you want me to do over there?" Klauber's answer surprised Murrow. CBS wanted Ed Murrow to be the network's new European director, the position held for the past seven years by Cesar Saerchinger. Saerchinger had resigned because he saw no future in broadcast news!

Many at CBS did not want to send Ed to Europe and lose a dynamic and successful director of talks. But William Paley insisted. He wanted an insightful person in Europe, someone who understood international affairs and had negotiating experience. CBS's rival network, the National Broadcasting Company (NBC), had two people in place already. Fred Bate was their European director and Max Jordan covered activities in Berlin. European broadcasting stations were governmentally controlled and many people overseas thought Bate and Jordan represented the United States government. CBS needed a forceful presence across the Atlantic.

Ed and Janet sat up all night discussing the offer. They finally decided that no matter what happened, living and working in London would be interesting. "As in almost everything we've done," Janet later told a reporter, "I felt that a new experience would be a lot of fun." For the rest of his life, Ed Murrow considered that decision to go to Europe the greatest one of his life. "It gave me a front-row seat for some of the greatest news events in history."

*Murrow in uniform, WWII (National Archives)*

## CHAPTER FIVE

# Eyewitness to History

*The opposing team has just crossed the goal line.*
—William L. Shirer

The First World War—"the war to end all wars"—ended in 1918 with Germany's total humiliation. Less than twenty years later, the world was on the verge of an even bloodier conflict. Hitler's rearmed Germany had positioned itself for revenge. Ed Murrow, through his IIE experiences resettling Jewish refugee scholars, was very much aware of the growing tensions in Europe. The Murrows sailed to Europe in April 1937, in First Class, excited, but well aware of the dangers ahead.

They looked forward to the change. "It wasn't anything that we were accustomed to," Janet Murrow explained. "We'd been married in '34 and everything had been on a temporary basis really, getting used to the IIE and then, getting used to CBS and [then] going to London."

In spite of looming war threats, Ed and Janet viewed the new job as a dream come true. Their arrival coincided with the coronation of England's new king, Edward VIII. With all the broadcast details for CBS already arranged by Cesar Saerchinger, they had nothing to do but act like tourists. They settled into a small apartment vacated by the Saerchingers and into a heady social life which quickly expanded beyond the circle of friends Ed had made during his IIE visits. In a short time, they moved to the slightly larger apartment they would live in throughout the upcoming war, at 84 Hallam Street, not far from the British Broadcasting Corporation (BBC) studios and the CBS European office.

The Murrows quickly adjusted to British life. "There were dense fogs at night," Janet recalled, "and Ed had to find his way home at night. There were a couple of times when he couldn't find it!" Along with the apartment, the Murrows inherited a live-in maid, "a little girl—she was still in her teens," Janet recalled. "[Betty Matthews] was a child of a mining family in Wales. She was not used to strangers like us [but] we got to know each other very well." Throughout their years in London, Betty was a member of the Murrow family. When Betty married, the Murrows made room in their apartment for her new husband.

Even as a college student, Murrow had been conscious of his appearance. In London, he discovered the famous tailors and styles of Savile Row. For the rest of his life, he had his suits made in London. "He hadn't spent as much money on things as he did in London," Janet remembered.

As Saerchinger's successor, Ed's job was to schedule interesting broadcasts to America about European life. "Arranging broadcasts from Europe," he explained, "was a leisurely, civilized sort of business, plenty of time to read and see your friends. It involved such things as relaying to this country the Vatican Choir at Eastertime, a speech by de Valera [Irish political leader], folk music from Scandinavia, the song of a nightingale in a Surrey wood."

But from the beginning, Ed Murrow knew he wanted to change the way Americans heard about Europe. Soon after arriving in London, Murrow paid a courtesy call on the British Broadcasting Corporation, upon whom CBS depended for studio and technical support. The head of the BBC, Sir John Reith, asked the newcomer, "Why did they send you here?"

"I really don't know," Murrow answered.

"Well," continued Sir John, "in view of your record, I dare-say your company's programs in the future will be a little more intellectual."

"On the contrary," Murrow disagreed, "I want our pro-grams . . . to be down to earth, in the vernacular of the man in the street."

Murrow spent his first year learning the ins and outs of international broadcasting while keeping current with the changing and ominous political conditions in Europe. He wrote, "If there is any trouble over here I, for one, intend to be watching it." He and Janet particularly enjoyed meeting and socializing with a wide variety of interesting and influen-tial people. In a letter to his mother in June 1937, Ed related, "All of these people have something to say and they introduce me to loads of people . . . they are also teaching me a lot about the human side of politics here. It's extraordinary."

He traveled throughout Europe to arrange programs, supervise engineers, and maintain relations with each coun-try's broadcasting authorities. He traveled so extensively and dressed so well, British customs agents once briefly detained and investigated him for the possibility that he might have been smuggling expensive ties! Thereafter, he arranged for a special diplomatic passport which allowed him free access in and out of the country.

He had to be inventive. While supervising a Bastille Day broadcast from Paris, he resorted to hand signals to coordinate three widely separated reporters caught up in a crowded, noisy square. A 1938 *Scribner's* magazine article described his frequent travels. "He lived in the air and in a suitcase and used the long distance telephone with the lavishness of a Hollywood film producer." On one occasion, his return home was curtly announced by Betty Matthews: "Mrs. Murrow, man's here again!"

Time differences and a lack of understanding by CBS personnel in New York of international protocol led to frequent conflicts with Murrow. In New York, the executives were leery of preempting regularly scheduled sponsored programs for coverage of unsponsored—and therefore unpaid— European news events. Once, when Murrow arranged to cover a scheduled state speech by the queen of the Netherlands, CBS responded with a telegram: WILL CARRY HER MAJESTY'S ADDRESS IF YOU CAN MAKE IT AN HOUR LATER.

For all his energy, Murrow found that Europe was too big for one person to cover. The cultural programs he arranged competed for his attention along with events in the ever-tense political arena. Hitler's growing military machine began to defy existing international treaties. In 1936, German troops marched into the previously demilitarized Rhineland area on France's border. In 1937, the Nazis turned their attention to neighboring Austria, the German-speaking country of Hitler's birth. Through assassination, bullying, and trickery, opposition to the Nazis was silenced and preparations for *Anschluss*, the political unification of Germany and Austria, were well under way. To bolster the CBS presence in Europe, Murrow hired an experienced newspaper reporter, William L. Shirer, as the network's Vienna, Austria–based "Continental Representative." Like Murrow, Shirer himself did not initially broadcast but only arranged for other newspaper reporters to explain and analyze the news. Shirer found it strange that his new job required him to hire others less qualified than himself to report on the political situation in Europe. At the same time, Murrow, who had no professional news background, was eager to broadcast, too. Writing to his brother, he expressed his longing. "I want to cover something myself," he said. "God, I know I could do it if I had the chance."

Shirer almost didn't get the job. His hiring, for what was initially only a management position, depended on an on-air audition and the bosses in New York did not like what they heard. They thought his high-pitched voice was not of broadcast quality and would not appeal to listeners. But Murrow, recognizing his new colleague's more important talents as a seasoned reporter who understood the political scene in Europe, insisted and CBS relented. "I wanted him for CBS knowing that he could do the job," Murrow told the New York executives. "He is a good linguist and is everything that radio news is not: sensitive to news events." Once Shirer was hired, Murrow and he began to plan coverage of the looming crises. Both understood that Austria would be the site of the next conflict.

To the cheers of thousands of waiting supporters, German troops crossed the border into Austria on March 12, 1938. The previous day, Shirer, on his way to the hospital where his wife awaited the birth of their first child, watched joyous mobs of sympathizers gather under seas of fluttering Nazi flags. As cries of "Heil, Hitler! Heil, Hitler!" reverberated throughout the city, Shirer understood that the German leader would soon arrive. He was witnessing an important news event as the only American radio reporter in the city, and had to get the story out. He tried, without immediate luck, to contact Murrow, who was in Warsaw, Poland, arranging a children's concert for the CBS program *American School of the Air*.

Later that day, Murrow returned Shirer's call. Fearful that the telephone line was tapped, Shirer used a prearranged signal to indicate what was happening. "The opposing side has just crossed the goal line," he said. "Are you sure?" Murrow asked. "I'm paid to be sure," Shirer firmly answered. Since all radio facilities now came under Nazi control, Shirer was unable to broadcast from Vienna. Murrow told Shirer to fly to London and broadcast his firsthand impressions to America from there. In turn, Murrow planned to fly from Warsaw to Vienna and take Shirer's place.

It was easier said than done. Flights out of Vienna to London and other European cities were overbooked by Jews fleeing for safety. But Shirer had no difficulty obtaining a flight to Berlin and there transferring to another plane for London, where he became the first CBS staffer to report on-air. Murrow, meanwhile, flew to Berlin but was unable to get a seat on any flight to Vienna. Desperate, he chartered a twenty-seven-seat Lufthansa airplane at CBS expense and arrived in the Austrian capital as its only passenger in time to witness Hitler's triumphant entrance into the city.

Back in New York, William Paley, the president of CBS, had a thought. Why not broadcast live from various European capitals to give American listeners a sampling of opinions about the Anschluss? Something like that had never previous-ly been attempted and his own engineers were skeptical. A message was sent to Shirer in London to make the necessary arrangements. Murrow, on the other end of a telephone line to the CBS office in London, organized the complicated plan by scheduling studio and transmitter facilities and lining up speakers in major capitals of Europe.

At eight o'clock on the evening of March 13, 1938, radio news reporting changed forever. CBS announcer Robert Trout told listeners that the regularly scheduled program would not be heard. "To bring you the picture of Europe tonight, Columbia now presents a special broadcast," he said, "which will include pickups direct from London, Paris, and other such European capitals. . . ."

Beginning in London with a report from William Shirer, who then introduced a member of the British Parliament for remarks, the broadcast moved on timed cues to correspon-dents in Paris and Berlin and then back to London. There, Shirer read a dictated report from their correspondent in Rome, who was unable to make arrangements for studio time. The half-hour program ended with a live report from Ed Murrow in Vienna.

It was Murrow's first official radio news broadcast and hinted at his future broadcasting style. He gave listeners a ver-bal portrait of what Vienna was like at that moment, begin-ning with his recent flight into the city. "From the air, Vienna didn't look much different than it has before," he began. Then, careful not to offend the German censors who moni-tored every word, he conveyed the feeling of near-joyful hys-teria among Austrians as they awaited Hitler's arrival. "They lift the right arm a little higher than they do in Berlin and the

*Heil, Hitler* is said a little more loudly. . . . There's a certain air of expectancy about the city, everyone waiting and wondering where and at what time Herr Hitler will arrive."

Across America, listeners felt as if they were eyewitnesses to history. Murrow's goal was to "make listeners feel what it is like. It's like I've been preparing for this my whole life." For the next ten days, CBS broadcast a succession of other roundup programs. Shirer and Murrow did not get much sleep. Neither did Americans, suddenly discovering the news potential of radio.

Most of the correspondents heard on those broadcasts were newspaper or news-service reporters. They did not work directly for CBS and had to obtain permission from their own employers to appear on the air. Murrow knew that if radio were to develop its own news programming, it could no longer depend on others for staffing.

On his return to London after the Anschluss crisis, CBS gave him permission to build a full-time European news staff. For the first time, a radio network would have its own correspondents stationed in key European cities. From the beginning, he hired a new breed of broadcast reporters. Collectively, they became known as "Murrow's Boys" and included the legendary broadcasters who made CBS the major broadcast news medium in the United States. Eric Sevareid, Bill Downs, Howard K. Smith, Richard C. Hottelet, and Winston Burdett provided American listeners with the best in news coverage and insight during World War II and for decades beyond.

As in his controversial selection of Shirer, he insisted that his correspondents have intimate knowledge of Europe and world events, a flair with words, and the ability to think on their feet. A good announcer's voice was not necessary. "I tried to concentrate on finding people who were young and knew what they were talking about . . . even though they might not win any elocution contests." Ed Murrow transmitted his views on reporting to New York. "I think we should try and develop a style of reporting that will go beyond anything that has ever been done before. Don't you think that by focusing in on people, narrowing down on how they live, we could then be saying a lot more about events than by merely reporting politics and economic news? I am interested in people—how they get by, the way they talk."

When the next Nazi-instigated crisis occurred six months later, CBS was set to cover it. In September 1938, Hitler announced that he was prepared to annex the Sudetenland, a section of Czechoslovakia inhabited largely by people of German heritage. France and Russia had signed pacts to defend Czechoslovakia, and Britain was expected to join with them if Germany attacked. During a month of negotiations and threats, the world anticipated the start of a major war, which no one except Germany seemed to want. People in the United States were confused by the onrushing tide of events.

At CBS headquarters in New York, veteran news commentator H. V. Kaltenborn literally moved a cot into the studio and remained on duty continually for eighteen days, analyzing each and every move during the crisis. In Europe, Murrow and Shirer both broadcast live and continued to arrange radio appearances by leading European political figures. During the Munich crisis, CBS provided 471 broadcasts or bulletins from eighteen world capitals, many aired live during the middle of the night to anxious Americans. Radio news had come into its own. CBS engineers developed independent "cue" channels so overseas correspondents could communicate off-air with New York and hear one another as they broadcast from far-flung sites.

On September 12, Hitler's address to the Nazi Congress was broadcast with English translation over CBS from 2:15 to 4:00 P.M. New York time. At the speech's conclusion, Kaltenborn said, "In substance, then, the speech was very belligerent. . . . On the whole, I should say that Europe will breathe more freely tonight. . . ." That evening, Edward R. Murrow provided his own analysis from London. "The feeling is fairly widespread in Britain that the British government will urge Czechoslovakia to do anything short of actually dismembering the country to prevent war."

During the first days of the crisis, Murrow adopted the opening previously used by his predecessor, Cesar Saerchinger: "Hello, America, this is London calling." A week later, he had reduced that opening to three words: "This . . . is London."

British Prime Minister Neville Chamberlain sought to defuse the crisis by visiting Hitler. Chamberlain, Hitler, Italy's Mussolini, and France's Daladier met on September 29, 1938, to sign an agreement known as the Munich Pact. The agreement effectively forced Czechoslovakia to give up territory to Germany. "Don't worry, Ed," Jan Masaryk, the Czech ambassador to London, told Murrow, ". . . there is a God." Upon his return to London, Chamberlain, waving the paper he said had brought "peace in our time," was acclaimed a hero.

During a broadcast from London on September 25, 1938, Ed Murrow told his listeners: "I just want to tell you that those of us here who talk to you from over here are fully conscious of our responsibility and propose to give you an undistorted picture of the history being made in Europe during these long days and nights. . . ." Sales of radio sets grew as listeners turned to radio news reports as never before. Almost overnight, Edward R. Murrow was known all over America. His sudden fame was described in *Scribner's* magazine. "He has more influence upon America's reaction to foreign news than a shipful of newspapermen."

When the Munich crisis ended, CBS was the preeminent source of broadcast news in the United States. A proud William Paley sent a congratulatory cable to Murrow and Shirer: COLUMBIA'S COVERAGE OF THE EUROPEAN CRISIS IS SUPERIOR TO ITS COMPETITORS AND IS PROBABLY THE BEST JOB OF ITS KIND EVER DONE IN BROADCASTING. To commemorate their broadcasting achievement, CBS published a glossy public relations booklet documenting its coverage of the Munich crisis. Beyond the statistics of broadcast hours and the number of stations that carried the programming was the recognition that CBS coverage had permanently altered radio news. There was little time to rest on the laurels of success. A year later, the Germans invaded Poland and the world was involved in the second global war of the century.

*Murrow, bombed out London building (CBS)*

# CHAPTER SIX

# This . . . Is London

*You laid the dead of London at our doors.*
—Archibald MacLeish

Germany's invasion of Poland on September 1, 1939, was a calculated move. Knowing that Britain and France were obligated to come to Poland's assistance, the Germans purposely escalated their ongoing invasions of neighboring countries into a full-fledged world war. On the other side of the Atlantic, President Franklin D. Roosevelt officially declared the neutrality of the United States. While Americans opposed involvement in a foreign war, they cast a wary eye on activities in Europe. Many Americans turned to their radios for the latest European news as the voices of isolationist politicians resounded across the country.

On September 3, 1939, Prime Minister Neville Chamberlain declared a state of war between Britain and Germany and shattered his promise of "peace in our time." Within a few days, a British Expeditionary Force was on its way to France to fight the Germans. With CBS executives basking in the glory of their earlier Munich-crisis coverage,

Ed Murrow continued to build an exclusive CBS staff of news reporters in Europe.

By the time Germany invaded Poland, CBS News was ready, with Murrow orchestrating all activities from London. The innovative daily news roundups continued to draw anxious listeners. The network was also not afraid to interrupt regularly scheduled programs and commercials for news bulletins. During the last week of August 1939, Murrow and his staff reported live over eighty times from Europe, often staying awake all night to allow for time differences between continents.

As Americans settled down as uneasy observers of a foreign war, they looked forward to the daily broadcasts of Edward R. Murrow from London. Murrow did not repeat the major war news of the day, which could be heard in any regular news broadcast. Instead, he used his calm, authoritative, and forceful voice—all the speaking tricks learned from Ida Lou Anderson—to make Americans feel what it was like to live in a country at war. He crafted his words carefully. Every turn of phrase and inflection was precisely planned and scripted to be read aloud. He found it easy to dictate to his secretary. In that way, he was able to preview and fine-tune his delivery. There was a difference, he quickly discovered, between writing for readers and for listeners. He wanted Americans to feel, not just hear. He said of England:

This is a class-conscious country. People live in the same small street or apartment building for years and never talk to each other. The man with a fine car, good clothes, and perhaps an unearned income doesn't generally fraternize with the tradesmen, day laborers, and truck drivers. He doesn't meet them as equals . . . but if he's caught in Piccadilly Circus when a siren sounds, he may have a waitress stepping on his heels and see before him the broad back of a day laborer as he goes underground.

He did not believe in shouting simplistic headlines over the air; he tried to evoke a mood. "London as usual is black tonight. One gets accustomed to it, but it can hardly be called pleasant," Murrow told his listeners. To describe the evacuation of children from London to the safety of temporary homes in the countryside, he resorted to an understated personal observation.

It's dull in London now that the children are gone. For six days I've not heard a child's voice. And that's a strange feeling. No youngsters shouting their way home from school. And that's the way it is in most of Europe's big cities now. One needs the eloquence of the ancients to convey the full meaning of it. There just aren't any more children.

When World War II began, CBS promised listeners "to deal honestly, accurately, and fairly with the news and its public discussion." Murrow told his newly hired staff, "You are supposed to describe things in terms that make sense to the truck driver without insulting the intelligence of the professor." With those words in mind, Murrow's reporters covered the lightning Nazi push into one European country after another. Meanwhile, Murrow told listeners about preparations taking place in Britain for expected German attacks. As British troops engaged the Nazis elsewhere on the Continent, Murrow described life in Britain.

"In many ways," he reported, "London on a wet Sunday afternoon in wartime resembles London on a wet Sunday afternoon in peacetime." Beyond the similarities, Murrow told Americans of British military and civil-defense preparations. He conveyed a sense of the routine boredom at London's air-raid control center. "The telephone operators, young girls who might have been college sophomores at home, sat at their instruments, knitting or reading. One was reading the life of Madame Curie, another Tolstoy's *War and Peace*. . . ." The calm was about to be shattered.

By mid-1940, Germany had occupied Denmark, Norway, Belgium, and Luxembourg. In June, just prior to the fall of France, British troops were forced to retreat to the French coastal village of Dunkirk. There was a real possibility that a sizable portion of the British Army would be killed or captured by the Germans. To avoid this irreparable loss, the British began an unparalleled rescue by sea. Naval and private vessels of every size and level of seaworthiness along the British coast were pressed into service for the perilous round-trip journey across the English Channel. Under constant attack by German planes, nearly 350,000 British and French soldiers were evacuated to safety, ready to fight again.

Murrow practiced what he preached as he covered the war from London by focusing on average people and everyday events. As he covered the evacuation of Dunkirk he told of "the sound of a shell-shocked mongrel brought back from Dunkirk by a couple of British sergeants." He also personalized the intense courage of the nearly defeated British troops through the story of a British airman Murrow noticed at a Royal Air Force base. The young man kept shouting responses to questions from friends. "What's the matter with him?"

Murrow asked. "Oh," was the response, "he was shot down over Dunkirk, landed in the sea, swam back to the beach, was bombed for a couple of hours, and came home in a paddle steamer. His voice sounds that way because he can't hear himself. You get that way after you've been bombed for a few hours." That story taught Americans a lesson on British resolve no routine newscast could ever give.

Once France was occupied and neutralized, Hitler turned his full attention to Britain. Before an invasion of England could begin, the Germans needed to neutralize Britain's air power to leave the British defenseless. Just three weeks after the fall of France, German planes began attacking British sea convoys and ports. Facing Germany alone, Britain had no alternative but to prepare for the worst. The official order of the day to all Royal Air Force pilots read as follows: "The Battle of Britain is about to begin. Members of the Royal Air Force, the fate of generations is in your hands."

From June through the end of August, the skies above England's coast provided the backdrop for daily air battles between Royal Air Force and German planes. The targets shifted from ship convoys to British airfields and aircraft factories. The bombings grew closer to London. To the surprise of the German aggressors, the outnumbered British pilots were able to destroy large numbers of attacking planes, thereby preventing an immediate invasion. Winston Churchill, who replaced Chamberlain as prime minister, said of the selfless British pilots: "Never in the field of human conflict was so much owed by so many to so few."

Murrow reported on the everyday resilience of the English people. He told listeners about London street cleaners, "most of whom fear a war and want little more than to keep working." As he observed casual strollers on the street he told of "one man who looked so baffled by a newspaper headline, he crumpled it up and tossed it away." When the first bombs fell on London, Murrow was there. On August 24, 1940, German bombers escalated the war by accidentally dropping bombs on London. The scream of air-raid sirens and the sight of people heading to underground shelters became part of London life. "This is Trafalgar Square. The noise that you hear at the moment is the sound of the air-raid siren. . . ."

The following night, Murrow began his broadcast by saying, "The damage done by an exploding bomb to windows in a given area is a freakish sort of thing." Then, he proceeded to give the folks back home an explosives lesson. The London blitz was on. Between September 1 and 6, intense air battles over England led to fears that a German invasion was near. But British pilots withstood the withering fire and shot down six hundred and seventy enemy planes while their losses numbered four hundred.

On the night of September 7, Edward R. Murrow and another reporter were on a trip to the English coast to report on preparations there. Diving for cover at the sight of hundreds of German bombers overhead heading for London, they became firsthand witnesses to an escalation in the Battle of Britain. Unwilling to risk the further dangers of daytime raids, the Germans chose to fly under cover of darkness. Reporting later, Murrow described what he had seen. "It was like a shuttle service, the way the German planes came up the Thames, the fires acting as a flare path. Often they were above the smoke. The searchlights bored into that black roof but couldn't penetrate it. . . . It grew cold. We covered ourselves with hay. The shrapnel clicked as it hit the concrete road near-by. And still the German bombers came."

From September to December 1940, London replaced the outlying airfields and factories as the prime German target. On average, one hundred and fifty German bombers flew over London each night. They rained indiscriminate death and damage upon the city's civilian population. Over thirteen thousand civilians were killed. In the month of October alone, more than seven thousand tons of bombs were dropped on London. The effect of this prolonged terror upon the citizens of London was reported to America in detail by Edward R. Murrow.

Murrow was not content to report from the relative safety of the basement studios of the BBC (perhaps not so safe, considering that the BBC building suffered a direct hit on December 8). He stood on rooftops during bombing raids and scurried around London in his little sports car as bombs fell around him. "I can't write about anything I haven't seen," he told a colleague. Throughout that entire period, he got little sleep and lost weight. His health deteriorated. But still, he carried on. He had some near misses with disaster but never sought the safety of air-raid shelters. He told another reporter, "Once you start going into the shelters, you lose your nerve."

His only concern was to report what he saw and felt. "You may be able to hear the sounds of guns off in the distance. Very faintly, like someone kicking a tub," he told his listeners. Unlike other reporters, he refused to rely solely on governmental press releases and tried to convey to his listeners the immediacy of what was occurring.

There are no words to describe the thing that is happening. A row of automobiles, with stretchers racked on the roofs like skis, standing outside of bombed buildings. A man pinned under wreckage where a broken gas main sears his arms and face . . . the stench of air-raid shelters in the poor districts.

About five minutes ago, the guns in the immediate vicinity were working. I can look across just at a building not far away and see something that looks like a flash of white paint down the side, and I know from daylight observation that about a quarter of that building has disappeared, hit by a bomb the other night.

Throughout, he made Americans feel the suffering of the British people. He told how, every day, people tried to carry on with dignity and determination despite indiscriminate death and destruction. "If the people who rule Britain are made of the same stuff as the little people," he broadcast, "the defense of Britain will be something of which men will speak with awe and determination so long as the English language survives."

This is a race, the bomb squad trying to take away the bombs that have already fallen, before the next consignment comes down . . . but the milk and morning papers continue to arrive.

After one raid, he told listeners of a visit he made to a local shop where he bought three flashlight batteries. "You needn't buy so many," the clerk admonished him, "we'll have enough for the whole winter." Murrow, referring to nearby bombed-out shops, asked, "What if you aren't here?" The clerk replied, "Of course, we'll be here. We've been in business here for a hundred and fifty years."

On August 16, 1940, Murrow recounted his impressions of a five-hundred-mile trip through the south of England.

Many times the sirens sounded and a few times we saw the bombs fall. There is something unreal about this war over Britain. . . . Yesterday afternoon I stood at a hotel window and watched the Germans bomb the naval base at Portland, two or three miles away. In the morning, I had been through that naval base and dockyard. . . . The naval officers, including the admiral, had been kind and courteous, but as I stood and watched huge columns of smoke and fire leap into the air, I thought some of those officers and men would no longer be of this world.

As the bombs fell, Murrow conveyed the mixed feelings of fear, courage, and bravado displayed by the common people of London. "No words of mine can describe the spectacle over London tonight," Murrow reported, "so I'll talk about the people underground. I visited eleven air-raid shelters in the West End of London during this raid."

Murrow knew that people became quickly desensitized to the nightly casualty figures. Once, after reporting on the heroic and dangerous work of London's firefighters, he tried to personalize the bravery with this description: "And back at headquarters I saw a man laboriously and carefully copying names in a big ledger—the list of firemen killed in action during the last month."

Murrow painted word pictures for Americans that conveyed more than press releases ever could about the proud determination and unity of the British people who alone defended democracy in Europe.

Coming home today we were stopped by a constable in a little village. . . . Suddenly from behind us we heard a police car
with a loudspeaker: "Clear the street for His Majesty, the
King. . . ." The police car was followed by a big maroon car
carrying the King and a couple of staff officers. Behind that,
another car and a lone policeman riding a motorcycle. That
was all. . . . For fifty miles I drove a little ten-horsepowered car
just behind the policeman who was just behind the King. . . . I
saw those country folk as the King saw them and he must
have been encouraged. They were a calm-looking, smiling lot
of people. . . . I wondered in what other country in this mad
world can a King, a dictator, or a head of state travel with as
little protection. The policeman on the motorcycle didn't
even have a pistol.

The Murrow apartment, which through some miracle was
never bombed during the entire Battle of Britain, became a
social center for reporters and visiting dignitaries. Janet and
Ed, like other Londoners, tried to forget about the dangers
around them by carrying on with their daily routines.
Because of the time differences between the United States
and Britain, Murrow usually finished his broadcasts to
America in the wee hours of the morning. Then, with other
reporters or government officials in tow, he would return to
his apartment, where Janet had sandwiches and drinks ready.
Janet never knew whom to expect. During the war, she wel-
comed to her home such personalities as Eleanor Roosevelt,
Mrs. Winston Churchill, and the American ambassador to
Great Britain.

Janet worked at the British Ministry of Information and
occasionally broadcast for Ed on "women's" issues. She also
worked with an American-based committee to send British

children to safety in the United States. She talked to the mothers and fathers about America and prepared the children for temporary lives away from their parents. The program ended sadly when one of the ships carrying a number of children was torpedoed by the Germans. In late 1940, she became active in Bundles for Britain, an organization devoted to collecting clothing and food in America for the British.

In a broadcast on September 23, 1940, Ed tried to describe some of the "normalcy" in his own neighborhood.

My own apartment is in one of the most heavily bombed areas of London, but the newspapers are on the doorstep each morning—so is the bottle of milk. When the light switch is pressed, there is light, and the gas stove still works, and they're still building that house across the street, still putting in big windowpanes. Today I saw shop windows in Oxford Street, covered with plywood. In front of one there was a redheaded girl in a blue smock, painting a sign on the board covering the place where the window used to be. The sign read OPEN AS USUAL.

In other broadcasts, Murrow extolled the bravery and calm of the British people. "Today I walked down a long street. The gutters were full of glass; the big red busses couldn't pull into the curb. There was the harsh, grating sound of glass being shoveled into trucks. In one window—or what used to be a window—was a sign. It read: SHATTERED—BUT NOT SHUTTERED. Nearby was another shop displaying a crudely lettered sign reading: KNOCKED BUT NOT LOCKED."

Day after day, Murrow's broadcasts did more to turn American public opinion in favor of Britain and American involvement in the fight for freedom than all the formal diplomacy. Many credit him with shifting American public opinion away from isolationism.

He tried to be objective, but it was obvious that Edward R. Murrow had deep affection for the British in their solitary struggle. He understood that the place of Americans was beside their English-speaking cousins in the fight against the Nazis. So it was not at all out of character for Murrow to openly chastise his fellow Americans in a New Year's Eve broadcast ushering in 1941.

Most of you are probably preparing to welcome the new year. May you have a pleasant evening. You will have no dawn raid as we shall probably have if the weather is right. You may walk this night in the light. Your families are not scattered by the winds of war. You may drive your high-powered car as far as time and money will permit. . . . You have not been promised blood and toil and sweat and, yet, it is the opinion of nearly every informed observer over here that the decisions you make will overshadow all else during this year that opened an hour ago in London.

Murrow did not immediately recognize the impact he had on American public opinion. Yet, each night, fifteen million Americans regularly tuned to his broadcasts and hung on to every word of the distant war most knew would eventually affect them. He began each broadcast simply with "This . . . is London." The manner in which he pronounced these three words, with a slight hesitation after "this," became his trademark. Today, CBS continues to use a variation of Murrow's words as its television aural logo, "This . . . is CBS."

As his reputation grew in the United States, he became

more of a celebrity in England. He was interviewed for American and British magazines and his broadcasts were reprinted in newspapers. In October 1940, the Overseas Press Club in New York recognized Edward R. Murrow as the reporter who did the most to contribute "toward the information of the American people and the formulation of American national policy in international relations."

After the war, Murrow said that the greatest dream of his life was "to escape to the woods. I could read books about history, declaim great orations to an audience of lumberjacks, and just think." That was only a dream; his real lifestyle took a harsh toll on his physical and emotional well-being.

In September 1941, he received the sad news that his beloved teacher, Ida Lou Anderson, died. Distraught, Ed openly wept. She was the model after whom he patterned his life. She, from her sickbed, had even instructed him on the most effective delivery of his broadcast's opening words, "This . . . is London," and what became his customary closing, "Good night and good luck," which he used for the rest of his career.

In the latter part of 1941, Janet and Ed returned to the United States for a well-deserved quiet time away from the war. Janet toured the country on behalf of Bundles for Britain while Ed occupied himself with CBS business. He still did not fully realize the impact his reporting had on Americans. To honor him, William Paley, president of CBS, arranged a gala dinner on December 2, 1941, at the Waldorf-Astoria Hotel in New York.

That evening, over one thousand important people gathered to pay tribute to Murrow, then thirty-three years old. In a live hookup over the CBS radio network direct from the ballroom, people all over America heard Archibald MacLeish, the

Librarian of Congress, eminent poet, and Pulitzer Prize winner, say:

You burned the city of London in our houses and we felt the flames that burned it. You laid the dead of London at our doors and we knew the dead were our dead—were all men's dead—were mankind's dead—and ours. Without rhetoric, without dramatics, without more emotion than needed be, you destroyed the superstition of distance and of time—of difference and of time.

So long as the American people are told and told truly and told candidly what they have to face, they will never be afraid. And they will face it.

Because you told them the truth and because you destroyed the superstition of distance and of time which makes the truth turn false, you have earned the admiration of your countrymen.

Ed and Janet were invited to the White House for an informal dinner with President and Mrs. Roosevelt the following Sunday, December 7, 1941. That morning, as Ed played a leisurely game of golf, he and the rest of America were stunned by news of the Japanese surprise attack on Pearl Harbor, Hawaii. Ed and Janet waited by their telephone that afternoon for the expected cancellation of their White House invitation. Instead, they were told to come along. The president did not dine with them, but Eleanor Roosevelt graciously served plates of scrambled eggs. As they prepared to leave, Ed was asked to stay behind and visit with the president.

While Janet left the White House alone, Ed sat on a bench in a darkened corridor outside the Oval Office as high-ranking military personnel came and went. Finally, after midnight, he was shown into the president's office. Roosevelt ordered up some sandwiches and beer and the two men talked. First, the president asked Murrow about his experiences in Britain. Then, Roosevelt's anger surfaced as the conversation turned to Pearl Harbor. The president banged his fist on the table and shouted, "On the ground, by God, on the ground!" as he recounted the destruction of planes at American airfields. The attack, he told Murrow, had been devastating. He told the reporter of the large number of casualties and ship losses that were unknown to the public at that time.

Dazed and confused, Murrow left the White House. Here was perhaps the most important story of his life and he didn't know what to do with it. The president had not sworn him to secrecy, yet revealing the grave details of the losses at Pearl Harbor would profoundly affect the entire country. Janet remembered that Ed "came back to the hotel room and walked up and down all night wondering whether he could tell the story or not. And he did not tell the story. He hoped he would write about it sometime but he didn't, ever." He didn't confide in Janet at that time, either, except to relate an incident he witnessed while waiting outside the Oval Office for the president. He was shocked to hear one officer turn to another and say, "Sir, you shouldn't be in charge of a boat, let alone the U.S. Navy!"

The next day, President Franklin Delano Roosevelt appeared before a somber Joint Session of Congress to declare a state of war between the United States and the Empire of Japan. In return, Italy and Germany declared war on the United States. Britain was no longer the sole combatant on the side of freedom. As the United States began to marshal its human and material resources for battle, Ed

Murrow traveled on a lecture tour throughout the United States. In Seattle, Washington, he was reunited with his parents for a short visit and returned to Washington State University as a triumphant hero. Eleven years after his graduation, Edward R. Murrow stood to address the entire student body, the proud faculty seated behind him. Later that spring, Ed and Janet Murrow returned to London.

# Edward R. Murrow
## *A Photographic Portfolio*

*Ida Lou Anderson, 1930 (WSU)*

*Ed and Janet in London,*
*Portrait, 1938 (WSU)*

*Murrow with parents, brother*
*at WSU, 1942 (WSU)*

*Above: Murrow, London, with censor (National Archives)*
*Below: Murrow in London, BBC (National Archives)*

*Ed and Casey bidding Janet farewell, 1947 (WSU)*

*Murrow broadcasting coronation, London 1952 (WSU)*

*Murrow in Korea, 1952 (WSU)*

*Murrow in* See It Now *studio, 1952 (WSU)*

*McCarthy holding newspaper (National Archives)*

*Murrow and Rickover,* See It Now *(National Archives)*

*Ed, Janet, and Harry Truman in Key West, 1957 (WSU)*

*Ed, Janet, and Casey at Glen Arden Farm, 1955 (WSU)*

*Ed and Casey roughhousing on the ground (WSU)*

*Ed, Casey, and tractor, 1956 (WSU)*

*Above: Janet, Ed, and Casey in Stockholm, 1959 (WSU)*
*Below: Murrow and Don Wilson taking oath (National Archives)*

*Murrow at Cabinet meeting, 1961 (WSU)*

*Murrow and Marian Anderson,* See It Now *(National Archives)*

*Murrow in Ghana with young reporters, 1962 (National Archives)*

*Murrow inside missile,* CBS Reports *(CBS)*
*With the end of* See It Now, *Murrow's television energies focused on* CBS Reports. *He is shown here preparing for his report, "Biography of a Missile."*

*Murrow and Ben Gurion, Israel, 1956 (CBS)*
*Murrow had a deep affection for Israel and visited for business and pleas-*
*ure on several occasions. Here he is shown during the filming of a* See It
Now *interview with Israel's first prime minister, David Ben-Gurion.*

*Murrow in Berlin, 1953 (CBS)*
*He was used to reporting from world "hot spots."*

*Murrow and Friendly in Control Room (CBS)*
No two people did more for television news than Edward R. Murrow
and Fred W. Friendly (on right). They differed from each other in style,
appearance, and behavior. Together, they complemented each other's
strengths. The control room background provided a sense of activity and
involvement. That was precisely what Murrow and Friendly intended
for their viewers.

*Murrow interviewing soldier in Korea (CBS)*
*Edward R. Murrow brought news events into American homes in a way everyone could understand. He presented the "big picture" by focusing on the words and actions of common people. His interviews with soldiers in Korea demonstrated the futility of that unwanted war.*

*Murrow in correspondent's uniform (National Archives)*

# CHAPTER SEVEN

# Orchestrated Hell

*Ed Murrow could make you feel a story.*
—Robert Trout

Officially, Ed Murrow was only one of hundreds of American war correspondents in London. But his previous broadcasts from Europe gave him near-legendary status. By the time he returned to his apartment in London, he was the most influential American in Europe. His unique style of broadcasting set him apart from the other radio journalists. Broadcast historian Erik Barnouw said Murrow's "style had a quiet dignity. It avoided stuffiness and also the condescension of folksiness. It abhorred the frenzied—it favored short, concise statements."

As the buildup of United States military forces in England began, high-ranking American officers and newly arrived reporters turned to Murrow for help in assessing the British view of the war. When CBS President William Paley arrived as a newly commissioned army officer, he was amazed at the number of important people Murrow knew. No door seemed closed to his star reporter. "He was the number-one American in London," Paley later said, "who was best posted on what was happening in England and Europe generally."

Murrow instituted a scheduled weekly radio commentary heard every Sunday evening. His analysis usually focused on how the war affected the lives of common people. Those broadcasts were eagerly awaited by millions in America throughout the war. CBS news reporter Alexander Kendrick described Murrow's influence this way. "When he said, 'This . . . is London,' he established the same kind of rapport with the American nation as Franklin D. Roosevelt did with his fireside chats." Continuing the practice begun in reporting the Battle of Britain, he put the listener right into the action. On August 30, 1942, to mark Britain's third year of war, he described the continuing hardship in a way people everywhere could understand.

Three years is long enough for you to forget what it was like to be able to buy and drive a new car, buy a new suit of clothes whenever you wanted it. . . . Three years is long enough for schoolboys to grow up and become soldiers but not long enough to permit you to forget the friends who have died.

Murrow began his December 13, 1942, broadcast in an almost melancholy way. By the time he finished, the world heard the first accounts of the Holocaust, the indiscriminate murder by the Nazis of Europe's Jews. Murrow's news sources were of unquestioned reliability. He not only had friends in the highest levels of government in Britain and the United States, but also among the intellectual Europeans he had met and befriended over the years.

One of the nice things about talking from London on Sunday night is that one can sit down, review the events of the week, study the reports coming in from all over the world, and then talk about whatever seems interesting. Sometimes it's like putting letters in a hollow log or talking to yourself in a dark room. But tonight it's a little different. One is almost stunned into silence by some of the information reaching London. Some of it is months old, but it's eye-witness stuff supported by a wealth of detail and vouched for by responsible governments. What is happening is this: Millions of human beings, most of them Jews, are being gathered up with ruthless efficiency and murdered.

Murrow's powerful words, later proven sadly accurate, did not influence official thinking at the time. Most Allied leaders thought the reports were greatly exaggerated. After all, Europe was fighting a terrible war, with heavy casualties on both sides. No one wanted to believe that the Nazis were systematically destroying an entire people.

In spite of his powerful broadcasts from the basement studios of the BBC in London, Murrow wanted to report from the actual action sites, as he had during the Battle of Britain. In the spring of 1943, he finally received permission to go to North Africa. His month with British and American troops at the battlefront gave listeners personalized glimpses of gritty reality. In one broadcast, he spoke of two typical young American soldiers he had met. "Neither one," he grimly reported, "came back from patrol."

He took listeners into battle. "You drive on and reach a point a couple of miles behind the British gun positions. You climb a hill. It is 3:30 on Wednesday morning. Twenty minutes later, a trail of chain lightning seems to run along the ground, stretching for five miles on either side of you; the barrage opening the British attack is under way. . . . The Germans filled the sky with flares; the red, blue, and green signal lights kept drifting in the slight breeze above the valley. It was cold—you shiver—but it isn't that cold."

In a time before television, Murrow painted a human picture of war for his listeners. "You know what fear is like when you see a German soldier sitting, smiling against a tank. He is covered with dust and he is dead. You know what it is like." A BBC war correspondent said Murrow's words gave listeners "a picture of what it felt like, what it smelled like, what it burned like . . . so you, the listener, were standing with him. You were beside him at the microphone." He accompanied soldiers into battle and conveyed what the war meant to them. "It is about the men, individually described, who are fighting in a war many knew would just keep going on and on and on."

He returned to London, physically exhausted and emotionally drained. Throughout his career, he seemed to go through similar cycles, pushing himself to the limit of endurance and then collapsing into a period of recuperation. In mid-1943, Murrow returned to the United States to visit and rest. He had an unusual job offer to think about. The British government had asked him, a foreigner, to become head of the British Broadcasting Corporation. While home, Murrow consulted with old friends from his IIE days, including Supreme Court Justice Felix Frankfurter. In the end, he realized the inappropriateness of an American heading the BBC, and declined the offer.

In June, Murrow returned to England on board the luxury liner *Queen Elizabeth*, converted for the duration of the war into a crowded troop carrier. He told listeners about the dangerous voyage and the jaunty outlook of the young American soldiers heading to England to prepare for the invasion of Nazi-occupied Europe.

The men looked more confident than when they had come aboard. After all, they had crossed the big ocean, hadn't been seasick, and the big adventure was beginning. . . . As the men stood in line waiting to go aboard the train, I heard one say, "I'm going to write my mother and tell her I crossed the ocean standing in line."

While deeply involved with reporting the progress of the war, Murrow continued to build a quality staff of broadcast reporters for CBS in Europe. By the end of 1943, there were nearly ten full-timers in place. Janet was also an accredited war correspondent and filled in for Ed when he was away. She later humbly referred to herself as "a second-rater" in comparison to her husband, but her broadcasts were received just as warmly as his. She concentrated on "women's" stories or holiday features. She also broadcast for the British, sometimes with unintended results. She recalled one program in which she talked about the Mississippi River. Several days later, a friend told her about a youngster who had enjoyed her talk but didn't quite understand why a river was called "Mrs. Simpson!"

Ed Murrow was never satisfied with reporting from a distance. When British and American bombers began their merciless mass bombings of Germany, Murrow knew he had to go. CBS President Paley was not quite so sure. Murrow was an important wartime asset to America and the network, and the casualty rate for bombing crews was high. Paley also did not want to lose a friend. Nonetheless, by the end of the war, Murrow had flown on twenty-five dangerous missions.

Janet Murrow vividly remembered the first time Ed headed off for a bombing run over Berlin. With Ed at an undisclosed Royal Air Force base, Janet stayed home to await news of that night's raid. By noon, there still was no word from Ed. Radio reports indicated that dozens of British bombers had been shot down. Janet was frantic. She called Ed's secretary, Kay Campbell. "Have you heard anything from Ed?" Janet asked. "No," an equally frantic Kay answered. "I was waiting for someone to ask me." Kay telephoned the secret number at the air base. To their great relief, they quickly learned that no reporters had gone on that run. Janet and Kay were both upset with Ed for not telling them. But Janet was philosophical. She understood her husband. "He wasn't worried about himself," she said, "so he didn't think we should be."

Major German cities were going up in flames. It was now the turn of Berlin, Hamburg, and Cologne to feel the effects of mass bombings Londoners had experienced at the hands of the Germans. In one of the most famous broadcasts of World War II, Ed Murrow recounted his flight on the night of December 3 aboard a British Lancaster bomber, designated "D—for Dog," to Berlin and back. His account of the terror-filled night was rebroadcast by the BBC and reprinted throughout the United States and Britain. It became known simply as Murrow's "Orchestrated Hell" broadcast.

This . . . is London. Yesterday afternoon, the waiting was over. The weather was right; the target was to be the big city. . . .

D for Dog eased around the perimeter track to the end of the runway. We sat there for a moment. The green light flashed and we were rolling—ten seconds ahead of schedule! The takeoff was smooth as silk. The wheels came up, and D-Dog started the long climb. As we came up through the clouds, I looked right and left and counted fourteen black Lancasters climbing for the place where men must burn oxygen to live. The sun was going down, and its red glow made rivers and lakes of fire on the tops of the clouds. Down to the southward, the clouds piled up to form castles, battlements and whole cities, all tinged with red. . . .

And then I was on my knees, flat on the deck, for he had whipped the Dog back into a climbing turn. The knees should have been strong enough to support me, but they weren't, and the stomach seemed in some danger of letting me down, too. I picked myself up and looked out again. It seemed that one big searchlight, instead of being twenty thousand feet below, was mounted right on our right wing tip. D-Dog was corkscrewing. As we rolled down on the other side, I began to see what was happening to Berlin. . . .

The small incendiaries were going down like a fistful of white rice thrown on a piece of black velvet. As Jock hauled the "Dog" up again, I was thrown to the other side of the cockpit, and there below were more incendiaries, glowing white and then turning red. The cookies—the four-thousand-pound high explosives—were bursting below like great sun-flowers gone mad. And then, as we started down again, still held in the lights, I remembered that the "Dog" still had one of those cookies and a whole basket of incendiaries in his belly and the lights still held us. I was very frightened. . . . The bomb doors were open. Boz called his directions, "Five left, five left" and then there was a gentle, confident, upward thrust under my feet and Boz said, "Cookie gone." A few seconds later, the incendiaries went and "D-Dog" seemed lighter and easier to handle. I began to reflect again that all men would be brave if only they could leave their stomachs at home. . . . Berlin was a kind of orchestrated hell, a terrible symphony of light and flame. It isn't a pleasant kind of war-fare—the men doing it speak of it as a job. . . . Men die in the sky while others are roasted alive in their cellars. Berlin last night was not a pretty sight.

In that raid alone, fifty British bombers did not return. Neither did two of the four war correspondents who accompanied them. The "Murrow luck" held. When Ed called Janet to announce his safe return, he was totally "shaken." In his broadcast just a few hours later, he recounted his thoughts as "D-Dog" returned to England. "My mind went back to the time I had crossed that coast in 1938, in a plane that had taken off from Prague. Just ahead of me sat two refugees from Vienna—an old man and his wife. The co-pilot came back and told them that we were outside German territory. The old man reached out and grasped his wife's hand. The work that was done last night was a massive blow of retribution for all those who have fled from the sound of shots and blows on the stricken Continent."

Allied plans for "D day," the invasion of Europe by Allied forces, continued amid the highest secrecy. The Germans knew the time was approaching, but not the exact time and place of the invasion. Ed Murrow, in London, spent much of his time planning for CBS coverage of that major event of the war. When "D day" finally arrived, CBS was ready. "Murrow's Boys" were deployed with the Allied troops in the air and at sea. Murrow himself was selected one of the American "pool" reporters locked in a guarded basement studio at the British Ministry of Information to report on the events as they were cleared by the military censors.

He was also given a unique honor. At 3:37 on the morning of June 6, 1944, Murrow's voice was heard throughout Europe reading General Dwight D. Eisenhower's Order of the Day. "Soldiers, sailors and airmen of the Allied Expeditionary Force," Murrow intoned, "you are about to embark on a great crusade. . . ." Just after midnight in the United States, CBS interrupted its network dance music program to tell listeners, "A bulletin has just been received from the London office of the Associated Press which quotes the German Transocean News Agency as asserting that the invasion of Western Europe has begun." The beaches of Normandy on the coast of France swarmed with Allied troops.

"This . . . is London," Murrow told listeners a few hours later. "Early this morning we heard the bombers going out. It was the sound of a giant factory in the sky. It seemed to shake the old gray stone buildings in this bruised and battered city beside the Thames." The battle had turned. For the Nazis, the end was beginning.

Although the focus of the war shifted to the Continent, the Germans did not forget London. Less than a week after "D day," the first of over eight thousand unpiloted German V1 rockets were launched against the British capital with resulting casualties in the thousands. The rockets were a new source of terror to the civilian population. Later that year, thirteen hundred improved V2 rockets killed and maimed thousands more. Murrow gave listeners a prophetic view of these new and terrifying weapons in a broadcast on November 12, 1944.

The significance of this demonstration of German skill and ingenuity lies in the fact that it makes complete nonsense out of strategic frontiers, mountains and river barriers. And, in the opinion of many able scientists, it means that within a few years present methods of aerial bombardment will be as obsolete as the Gatling gun.

Janet, who had worked tirelessly for Bundles for Britain, undertook a new job at the behest of the American ambassador for the British-American Liaison Board. The board was established to ease the friction between the British and the hundreds of thousands of young American military personnel who found themselves strangers in a foreign land, and sometimes forgot their manners.

In September 1944, Murrow was aboard a United States cargo plane ferrying paratroopers to Holland. This was certainly not his first military flight, but it was the first on which he carried a tape recorder. CBS had forbidden the use of recording devices in its broadcasts. Murrow, who thought the policy foolish, included portions of his recording of men parachuting into Holland in his September 17 broadcast.

I look back at the door, and the pilot gives me the clenched-hand salute, like a boxer about to jump. . . . There's a burst of flak. You can see it right from the side. . . . Now every man is out. I can see their chutes going down now. Every man clear. They're dropping just beside a little windmill near a church, hanging there. Very gracefully. They seem to be completely relaxed, like nothing so much as khaki dolls hanging beneath a green lampshade. . . .

That fall, Ed Murrow received an honor that signaled the acceptance of radio news as a valid form of journalism equal to newspapers. The Association of American Correspondents in London elected him president, the first time a nonprint journalist had been so recognized. In September, Janet, who as an accredited war correspondent could easily travel, returned to the United States for a visit with her ill, elderly parents. Ed, emotionally and physically drained, carried on with his broadcasts. He tried to show listeners the changes he was beginning to notice as the war situation improved for the Allies.

There is a dim light in Europe now. The blackout is gradually lifting. And when I leave this studio tonight, I shall walk up a street in which there is light, not much, but more than there has been for five and a half years. You come to know a street pretty well in that time—the hole in the wooden paving blocks where the incendiaries burnt themselves out, the synagogue on the right with the placard which has defied four winters. . . . It is a street where in '40 and '41, the fires made the raindrops on the window look like drops of blood on a mirror. It's an unimportant street where friends died, and those who lived had courage to laugh.

He missed his wife and wrote and called her often. In November, Ed and Janet were reunited in New York. Ed spoke to news groups around the country about the state of the war and then they headed off to a Texas dude ranch for a quiet and relaxed vacation together. By the time they returned to London in February 1945, the war had taken a definite turn. The Allies were poised to advance into Germany.

In the spring, Ed moved through Germany with General George Patton's Third Army. On April 12, the day Franklin D. Roosevelt died, he was one of the first Americans to reach the liberated Buchenwald concentration camp. He was struck with horror at what he saw. Three days later, he sat in a studio, his tense body shaking with inner rage, and told the world what he had seen.

Permit me to tell you what you would have seen, and heard, had you been with me on Thursday. It will not be pleasant listening. If you are at lunch, or if you have no appetite to hear what Germans have done, now is a good time to switch off the radio, for I propose to tell you of Buchenwald. . . . There surged around me an evil-smelling horde. Men and boys reached out to touch me; they were in rags and the remnants of uniform. Death had already marked many of them, but they were smiling with their eyes. . . . When I entered, men crowded around, tried to lift me to their shoulders. They were too weak. Many of them could not get out of bed. I was told that this building once stabled eighty horses. There were twelve hundred men in it, five to a bunk. The stink was beyond all description. . . . In another part they showed me the children, hundreds of them. Some were only six. One rolled up his sleeve, showed me his number. It was tattooed on his arm. D-6030, it was. The others showed me their numbers; they will carry them till they die. . . . There were two rows of bodies stacked up like cordwood. They were thin and very white. Some of the bodies were terribly bruised, though there seemed to be little flesh to bruise. . . . Murder had been done at Buchenwald. . . . I pray you to believe what I have said about Buchenwald. I have reported what I saw and heard, but only part of it. For most of it I have no words. . . . If I've offended you by this rather mild account of Buchenwald, I'm not in the least sorry.

CBS reporter Charles Collingwood, one of "Murrow's Boys," later said that what Murrow saw that day in Buchenwald "remained with Ed and haunted him. It was something which affected him, I would guess, for the rest of his life." Germany formally surrendered on May 7, 1945. The next day, Murrow reflected on the previous six years. "The price of victory has been high. We don't yet know just how high—how many twisted minds, how much loss of faith and hope." He then alluded to America's place in the postwar world. "We have the power. Europe has no doubt that America is mighty in battle. Our nation, which was created by men who wanted to leave Europe, is the center of the hopes and some of the fears of millions who are in Europe today."

Murrow was given the prestigious Peabody Award for Excellence in Reporting, "as one who has done more for a new craft than any other practitioner." He commuted for a few months between New York and London to finish up his broadcasting responsibilities and to assure a smooth takeover by his successor, Howard K. Smith. Ed had a lot of thinking to do about his personal future. There were a number of job opportunities both in and out of broadcasting. But, yielding to pressure from CBS President Paley, Ed reluctantly accepted a promotion to the position of vice president and director of public affairs of CBS in charge of all news programming. He really did not want a management position, but took it out of a sense of loyalty to his friend Paley. *Newsweek* magazine intoned, "A brilliant broadcasting career is over."

On March 10, 1946, Murrow broadcast his last program from London. In tribute, BBC engineers presented him the microphone he had used for most of his *This . . . Is London* broadcasts. A few days later, the Murrows flew home. Ed Murrow, weary of war but looking forward to the future, returned to New York close to nine years after leaving for England. Now, he and Janet had not only to adjust to the unfamiliar vibrancy of New York, but to their new life as a family. Two Murrows left for London in 1937; three returned. Their son, Casey, was born in London on November 5, 1945.

Years later, Janet recalled how much Ed disliked being a vice president. During his short tenure in management, others at the network pointed with pride at the new programs and directions he initiated. *As Others See Us* and *You Are There* were innovative for their time. When he created a nightly news program featuring Robert Trout, *Newsweek* magazine wrote it was "one of the most carefully prepared news programs ever to hit the air. The first brainchild Edward R. Murrow has put on the air since he became CBS head." Still, Murrow was not happy. "It's the big desk with the telephones," he complained, "the In basket and the Out basket. Conferences, memos, budgets, and firing people. Who am I to be firing people, the Almighty himself?" When he was forced to fire his old colleague William Shirer, he grew even more depressed. Paley, realizing the mistake of removing Murrow from the air, relented and supported his return to news reporting.

In the fall of 1947, Murrow gave up the vice president's plush office and replaced Robert Trout on the nightly news show. The new program, now called *Edward R. Murrow with the News*, operated under strict rules dictated by Murrow and gladly agreed to by CBS. There were to be no commercial messages from the sponsor, the Campbell Soup Company, during the program, only at the beginning and end of the broadcast. The fifteen-minute program began with Murrow delivering the news and ended with a six-minute commentary. He felt strongly that there had to be a clear distinction to the listener between "ascertainable fact" and "analysis" of the news. Toward the end of each broadcast the announcer said, "Mr. Murrow will be back in a moment with his word for the day." Then, after the commercial message, Murrow read a short quotation he thought relevant to the day's news. The program closed with his classic, "Good night and good luck."

Preparations for the fifteen-minute broadcast kept Murrow occupied for most of the day. After working with his staff in selecting the day's stories, he then spent two to three hours dictating or typing his commentary. "I'm slow at the job,"

Murrow told a reporter, "because I visualize every sentence before I type the first letter." He developed a consistent work schedule, built around the demands of the nightly news program.

As airtime approached, he grew increasingly nervous. When he began to speak on-air, his calm, steady, and reassuring voice gave no indication of the near-panic that nightly enveloped him during the broadcast. Under the table, his feet maintained a continual nervous bounce. Closer to the microphone, his face froze into rigidity as beads of sweat formed on his forehead. When the announcer ended the program with "Listen to Murrow tomorrow," Ed slumped in his chair, exhausted by the ordeal. As much as being on-air drained him physically and emotionally, he was drawn to the microphone. During his first year on the air, he won three major broadcasting awards. In 1949, in recognition of his value to the network—but much to his amusement—he was elected to the board of directors of CBS.

Ed now had a small, spare office furnished with network-issue desk and chairs and a special stand-up desk, similar to one used by Winston Churchill during the war. Gone were the fancy trappings of a network vice president: Murrow couldn't have been happier.

*Murrow and Fred Friendly, 1953 (WSU)*

# CHAPTER EIGHT

# See It Now: Television News

*Ed was a teacher . . . helping others to understand so that they might make better choices.*
    —Dr. Jonas Salk

Ed Murrow's life changed the moment he met Fred W. Friendly. Friendly first approached Murrow with an idea to create a sound history of world events from 1933 to 1945. Murrow would narrate the recordings using the actual voices of the famous people who made the news. The first *I Can Hear It Now* recording became an overnight success and was quickly followed by two others. They were the first nonmusical records to become best-sellers. Critic Howard Taubman wrote in the *New York Times*, "Mr. Murrow is the narrator, and his comment not only holds the parade of aural history together but adds dignity and meaningfulness to the album."

The idea was then transformed into an hour-long radio show. *Hear It Now*, produced by Friendly and hosted by Murrow, was as popular as the original recordings. As television grew in popularity, the program evolved into *See It Now*, the new medium's first attempt to report on political and social themes. Murrow and Friendly knew nothing about television and learned through "on the job" trial and error. Friendly was a big bear of a man whose brashness and daring often intimidated staffers into technical and programming innovations that set the standard for the television industry. They were a unique team, drawing on each other's strengths to create television news. Years later, Friendly said, "I absorbed all Ed's values. Every scrap of film I edited, I edited with his eyes. Everything I wrote, I wrote with his fingers."

The first *See It Now* program was broadcast live on November 18, 1951. An announcer explained that the new program was "a document for television based on the week's news," then intoned, "Now, speaking from the actual control room of Studio 41, is the editor of *See It Now*, Edward R. Murrow." Murrow, sitting before television monitors, looked straight out at the viewers and explained the program's purpose and style.

This is an old team trying to learn a new trade. When we started this series of programs, we had to decide where to do it from. We decided to do it right here from the studio. My purpose will be not to get in your light anymore than I can, to lean over the cameraman's shoulder occasionally and say a word which may help to illuminate or explain what is happening. . . . We are, as newcomers to this medium, rather impressed by the whole thing. . . .

The program continued with a technological wonder as cameras allowed viewers to gaze simultaneously upon live pictures of the Atlantic and Pacific oceans. Then, switching to a more serious theme, Murrow narrated a portrait of American soldiers in Korea, involved in a war few at home understood. The cameras zoomed in on the faces of the young soldiers and captured their comments and feelings about being so far from home. At the end of the segment, Murrow looked into the camera to give viewers an update on the soldiers they had just met and the frontline action they were experiencing. He spoke solemnly of the casualties they suffered and ended by telling Americans, "They may need some blood. Can you spare a pint?" He turned his face away from the camera quickly as if to make the question appear undebatable. Over the next few days, hundreds of thousands of viewers turned up at Red Cross centers to donate blood.

Just as he had used radio to bring World War II into American living rooms, he now used television to bring home the grim realities of yet another war. As in radio, he always focused attention on the small details to help people understand the larger story. Murrow's *See It Now* began with a report from Korea. He headed there for the next two Christmases to make in-person reports on the war. For the 1952 Christmas-in-Korea program, he and Friendly assembled a crew of fifteen photographers and reporters. For the most part, the filming of *See It Now* programs was unscripted and the camera crews were instructed to focus on close-up shots and shoot much more film than would actually be needed. On one of the Korean trips, seventy-seven thousand feet of film was ultimately edited down by Friendly to six thousand.

The 1953 visit to Korea opened with a seemingly unending scene of a soldier trying to shovel a foxhole out of the frozen Korean soil. All that was heard was the repetitious clang of the metal blade of the shovel striking the rocky ground. Murrow and Friendly used the actual sounds of the scenes they filmed. After what seemed a long time, Murrow simply said, "This is Korea, where a war is going on. That's a marine, digging a hole in the ground. They dig an awful lot of holes in the ground in Korea. This is the front. Just there, the no-man's land begins, and in the ridges over there, the enemy positions can be clearly seen. In the course of the next hour, we shall try to show you around Korea a bit."

For the rest of the program, Murrow and his reporters interviewed American soldiers throughout the country, focusing on the routine tasks of men at war. Murrow summarized the overall message of the hour clearly: "There is no conclusion to this report from Korea because there is no end to the war."

Murrow brought the Korean War home to Americans. Not until the Vietnam War two decades later would television play such an important role in defining American participation in a war few Americans really understood or wanted. The description of Murrow's Korea broadcasts in *Variety*, the entertainment industry's trade newspaper, could be validly applied to the role of television news in reporting the Vietnam War. "What Murrow saw in Korea, we saw, for a battlefront was brought into the parlor."

Murrow drew on his own prestige at the network as Friendly bullied his way through layers of bureaucracy, in Murrow's name, to assemble an independent team of reporters, camera, and technical people for the exclusive use of *See It Now*. Of course, Murrow still had full access to the worldwide staff of CBS network correspondents, most of whom he originally hired. Under Friendly's demanding direction, the staff worked at a grueling pace to produce three or four program segments each week. Murrow was heavily involved not only with *See It Now* but with his nightly radio news program and other commentary pieces.

During its seven years on the air, the program's format gradually evolved. As program segments were cut, broadcast times changed, and the frequency of programs diminished, Murrow and Friendly's original goals remained unchanged. Alexander Kendrick said, "Their emphasis was on human beings affected by events, rather than on the events themselves."

Murrow instructed the staff always to remember "simplicity of presentation" and to look for the "little picture." Unknown people caught up in events beyond their control received the same treatment as famous writers, artists, and musicians. Grandma Moses, Carl Sandburg, and Louis Armstrong appeared on *See It Now*. Sandburg even sang a chorus of his favorite Civil War song, "Eating Goober Peas." Dr. Jonas Salk, inventor of the life-saving polio vaccine that bears his name, became Murrow's friend after his appearance on the program. Murrow flew in an air force plane through the eye of a hurricane and spent time traveling the famous Orient Express railway through Europe.

While the early programs were informative, most were not controversial. Soon, Friendly and Murrow, to the regret of CBS executives, began to realize the unique power of television to illuminate events. Murrow watched as the fear generated by Senator Joseph McCarthy's reckless accusations took hold of America. The "Red Scare" gripped the country in a vise of fear. A "wrong" thought or an "incorrect" point of view could subject a person to charges of disloyalty and treason. People were dismissed from jobs they had held for years because of rumor or false accusation. Unproven accusations were undermining American democratic principles. This was too great an issue for Murrow to ignore. Indeed, a number of Murrow's acquaintances in broadcasting, the arts, and government had lost their jobs because of political views or unproven charges.

Friends and colleagues urged him to use his powerful voice to speak out. But Murrow patiently waited for just the right opportunity to stir public consciousness on McCarthyism. One day in October 1953, Ed Murrow was leaving the CBS building as Fred Friendly was coming in. "Here, read this," Murrow said, "it might be our case history," and handed Friendly a news clipping from a Detroit newspaper. It was the story of a young lieutenant ordered to resign his commission from the air force because his father and sister were suspected of being Communist sympathizers.

First Lieutenant Milo Radulovich adamantly refused to resign. Murrow and Friendly sent a producer to Michigan to meet Radulovich and review the transcript of the air force hearing. According to the transcript, Radulovich's loyalty "was not, in any way, the question." Rather, it was the charge that his father and sister read "subversive newspapers" and engaged in otherwise undocumented "highly suspicious activities." A *See It Now* camera crew was quickly dispatched to interview Radulovich, members of his family, and neighbors. The air force was invited to respond in a filmed interview, but refused. Instead, two high-ranking officers were dispatched to New York to dissuade Murrow from making the broadcast.

Murrow and Friendly, after viewing the films, decided to devote the entire half-hour of *See It Now* on October 20, 1953, to the Radulovich story. While CBS executives did not attempt to censor the program, they refused to advertise it. Friendly and Murrow pulled out their personal checkbooks to pay for a single advertisement in the *New York Times*. The ad, without the usual CBS logo, simply announced, "The Case Against Milo Radulovich, A0589839, produced by Edward R. Murrow and Fred W. Friendly." It was not the last time both men would dig into their own pockets to advertise a *See It Now* program because the network was unwilling to support its own program. "It was just that when we would get something very good," Friendly later observed, "you know the feeling, when you're bursting over it, it's so good—you want to make sure everybody sees it."

The five hours of filmed interviews were carefully edited over ten days to fit the half-hour time slot. The Milo Radulovich viewers saw was loyal and conscientious—a "typical American"—caught up in a horrible situation beyond his control. No evidence could be found that his father or sister was a Communist. The commander of the local American Legion summed up the feelings of many when he said, "If it comes to the point where you and I are held responsible for the activities . . . of our families, then we better all head for cover." The articulate young lieutenant asked if his children "are going to be judged on what their father was labeled? Are they going to have to explain to their friends et cetera, why their father's a security risk? . . . I see a chain reaction that has no end to anybody—for anybody." The program ended with a close-up of Murrow.

We believe that "the son shall not bear the iniquity of the father," even though that iniquity be proved; and in this case, it was not. But we believe, too, that this case illustrates the urgent need for the armed forces to communicate more fully than they have so far done, the procedures and regulations to be followed in attempting to protect the national security and the rights of the individual at the same time. . . . And it seems to us that—that is, to Fred Friendly and myself—that that is a subject that should be argued about endlessly.

The furor created by the program was dramatic. Most viewer mail and telegrams overwhelmingly supported Radulovich, but conservative political groups were angered. For Murrow, this was just the first step toward a program on Senator McCarthy himself.

The November 24 program of *See It Now* opened with a special guest, the secretary of the air force. Five weeks after the Radulovich program, the secretary announced that he had reviewed the case and "directed that Radulovich be retained in his present status in the United States Air Force." The program continued with "An Argument in Indianapolis," about the right of the American Civil Liberties Union to rent a meeting hall in that city. The Minute-Women of Indiana and the American Legion accused the ACLU of trying to "overthrow our government by force and violence, as well as by infiltration." They simply did not want the ACLU to meet. The filmed interviews were emotional. In response, an ACLU attorney said, "And so in civil liberties we find strange folks side by side who disagree on anything with everybody except on the right of those who disagree with them to be heard."

In the end, a Roman Catholic priest offered his church's social center as a meeting site. "That so many people are so quick to take the law into their own hands," Father Gossens said, "I should say perhaps, to ignore the law and to deny others the right to peaceful assembly and free speech—somebody has to take a stand on the subject and prove to them that they are, in their activities, actually un-American in their way of procedure. . . . And if the church and religion do not uphold those basic principles which come from God, then who will?" After those brave and powerful words, there was nothing more for Ed Murrow to say. He closed the program simply: "That was the argument in Indianapolis last week. Good night and good luck."

As Murrow headed off on what was becoming a yearly wartime visit to Korea, he told his staff to gather material for a program on Senator Joseph McCarthy. Janet remembered Ed coming home one night and grimly announcing, "Well, we've decided to go ahead with the program." The time had finally come. By the time he returned, the staff under Friendly's direction had done its job.

Unfortunately, Murrow could not get back to New York at once, but went directly from the plane to a hospital. As frequently happened during his life, he had again pushed himself into a state of near total exhaustion. But the McCarthy program aired on March 9, 1954, followed a week later by the report of Annie Lee Moss's appearance before McCarthy's Senate committee.

Assuming there would be a vicious personal attack on him by McCarthy, CBS hired a team of attorneys and investigators who virtually dissected and cataloged every word Murrow ever wrote or broadcast. They were looking for anything McCarthy might use that could even remotely connect Murrow to any subversive activities. File cabinets of reports, studies, and old scripts held everything they found. McCarthy was not a foe to be taken lightly.

Murrow continued to work almost compulsively. He went to sleep in the early hours but arrived back at work by ten or eleven in the morning. He smoked continuously and did not think too much about food. Although he was now financially well off, Murrow never affected the lifestyle of the rich and famous. He always enjoyed reminding people of his humble roots. He was known to go to the finest gourmet restaurants and order a simple plate of scrambled eggs. "I think he was conscious of the effect that he made," Janet later remarked, "but sometimes he would just like to have scrambled eggs. So he would order it and he didn't mind that it made that impression that he was criticizing."

As if *See It Now* and his regular evening radio news show were not enough to occupy his time, Ed was also involved in other regularly scheduled programs. *This I Believe* exceeded other radio shows in popularity. The daily five-minute show featured important personalities, introduced by Murrow, who talked about their personal philosophies. It was carried by nearly two hundred stations and appeared in syndicated newspaper columns. A book that included selections from the program, with an introduction by Murrow, sold over three hundred thousand copies.

Murrow's most popular television program was the weekly *Person to Person*, which first aired on October 2, 1953. It was not a news show, although important people were featured. For six years, Ed Murrow "visited" five hundred celebrities in their homes through the wonder of television technology. Today, live remotes by television are commonplace; in the 1950s they were almost unknown.

Each week, Murrow sat in his studio and conversed with celebrities in their own homes. The programs were scripted informally so guests could move about their homes, pointing out paintings on walls and prize possessions. Actually, the programs were highly structured. For days prior to the broadcast, the guest's home was invaded by dozens of technicians; camera, light, and sound crews; and miles of cabling. Since the program was live, Ed had to be prepared for any eventuality including storms, power failures, and suddenly fear-struck guests. Minutes before the show began, staff on location made sure that all telephones and televisions in the house were turned off. During one program, the blaring sirens of passing fire engines were clearly heard over the guests' voices.

Murrow had to employ acting skills, which his son, Casey, said "must have been incredibly difficult" for him. His guests could not see him during the *Person to Person* interviews. Viewers at home saw Murrow sitting in a comfortable chair, one leg crossed over the other, the omnipresent lit cigarette in one hand, smiling and nodding at a guest miles away. Murrow was actually looking into a blank hole with a small television monitor hidden from viewers. As Casey remembered, "When he was smiling cheerfully at the Smiths sitting on a couch he's actually looking at someone holding cue cards and the cue cards would have key words for the next question—he would not necessarily ask that question, trying to go with the flow of the conversation.

"He had an incredible memory," Casey added. "He could remember a twist of phrase—the way you said something: that way you said something different . . . and I think it was a real gift." That "gift," together with Ida Lou's training and his childhood-honed storytelling skills, gave his programs a sophisticated feel no other reporter could duplicate.

From Cedric Adams to William Zorach, the program was

an alphabetical encyclopedia of who was who in American politics, arts, sports, and entertainment during the 1950s. Among the over two hundred and fifty guests Murrow interviewed from 1953 to 1959 on *Person to Person* were singers Frank Sinatra, Rosemary Clooney, and Mahalia Jackson, actress Marilyn Monroe, humanitarian Eleanor Roosevelt, comedian Groucho Marx, boxer Rocky Graziano, baseball player Roy Campanella, conductor Leopold Stokowski, and the then Senator John F. Kennedy. Murrow, ironically, did several well-documented programs on the health hazards of smoking. The lessons he presented did not at all affect him and the sight of a lit cigarette dangling between his fingers had become his most familiar trademark.

He carefully prepared for all his shows. He recognized his lifelong problem with spelling and grammar and relied on others to polish up his scripts. Charles Kuralt, who later became a famous correspondent, began work at CBS as a news editor. Once, when temporarily assigned to Murrow, Kuralt reviewed a particular script and found a grammatical error. How could he tell the broadcasting legend there was a mistake? "It's wonderful, Mr. Murrow," Kuralt told Murrow. "I just wondered about this one word." Murrow glanced down. He fixed it with a few strokes of his pen. Then he looked up and nodded. "Good catch," he told the awestruck young man.

As financially rewarding as *Person to Person* was, *See It Now* was his serious and more worthwhile program. In the years since the inception of *See It Now*, changes in the broadcast industry began to clash with Murrow's deep-seated beliefs about the role and responsibility of broadcast journalism. By the mid-1950s, the power of commercialism and light enter-

tainment, such as quiz shows, began to encroach upon network journalism. Murrow, unwilling to lower his standards to
the commercial will of the CBS executives, witnessed the
gradual erosion of *See It Now*'s broadcast time. There were
problems attracting sponsors for the program and by the end
of the 1956–57 season, *See It Now*, its program standards
undamaged, appeared only irregularly.

Murrow traveled extensively to interview controversial
world leaders for *See It Now*. Janet often accompanied him.
Early in 1956, they traveled to Israel, one of several trips he
made there. He visited the legendary David Ben-Gurion,
Israel's first prime minister, and reported on the Arab-Israeli
crisis. Murrow returned to the Middle East a few months later
when the crisis erupted in all-out war.

Later that year, the legacy of McCarthy still hovering over
America, Murrow traveled to Burma to interview the leader
of Communist China, Chou En-lai, who was visiting there.
The State Department and President Dwight Eisenhower
were publicly critical, since no diplomatic relations existed
between the United States and the Communist country. Janet
accompanied Ed on a trip to interview Harry Truman in Key
West, Florida. "Ed thought highly of Mr. Truman," Janet
recalled, and was "delighted" to spend the time, on and off
camera, with the feisty former president.

*See It Now* ended. The last program, "Watch on the Ruhr,"
about the cold war in Germany, aired in mid-1958. Ed
Murrow, disappointed and tired, seriously considered leaving
broadcasting. For a while, he thought of running for the
United States Senate from New York or becoming the president of a college. But in his heart he knew these choices
would not really make him happy. He still had *Person to Person*,

the radio news program, and was beginning a new television show. *Small World*, technically advanced for the time, brought together guests from around the world to discuss major issues with one another by telephone while camera crews recorded the action at each location. He was busy but still felt unhappy and unfulfilled.

In 1959, *CBS Reports* was created to fill the void left by *See It Now*'s removal from the air. The one-hour investigative reports, produced by Fred Friendly but under the direct control of CBS News, provided in-depth views on newsworthy topics. Before leaving for a year away, Murrow recorded the narration for the first *CBS Reports* program, "Biography of a Missile." When he returned, his appearances on the program were infrequent but memorable. The program which evoked the most response of any in the *CBS Reports* series was "Harvest of Shame," purposely scheduled by Murrow for the day after Thanksgiving, November 25, 1960. The program dealt with the terrible working and living conditions of agricultural migrant workers in the United States. "Harvest of Shame" led directly to governmental intervention to improve the lives of migrant farm workers and their families.

The *CBS Reports* theme music, "Fanfare for the Common Man," by Aaron Copeland began and the program opened dramatically with a scene of men calling out for workers to pick fruit and vegetables in the fields. Murrow explained:

This scene is not taking place in the Congo. It has nothing to do with Johannesburg or Cape Town. It is not Nyasaland or Nigeria. This is Florida. These are citizens of the United States, 1960. This is a shapeup for migrant workers. The hawkers are chanting the going piece rate at the various fields. This is the way humans who harvest the food for the best-fed people in the world get hired. One farmer looked at this and said, "We used to own our slaves. Now we just rent them."

It was vintage Murrow. While working on the program, Ed wrote to his brother, "It's like the old days, for I am actually sitting here helping to put together this fine document: should make some folks mad." Indeed, the network executives were not happy with yet another controversial Murrow program that embarrassed important CBS advertisers. Murrow, the legend, seemed almost out of place in the new profit-and-ratings-driven world of network broadcasting.

*Ed and Casey fishing in Wisconsin, 1957 (WSU)*

# CHAPTER NINE

# Off Camera

*Well, we have done as much damage as we can do.*
*How about a drink?*
                    —Edward R. Murrow

"This just might do nobody any good," the speaker began. All eyes in the ballroom of Chicago's Sheraton-Blackstone Hotel focused on the legend before them. The members of the Radio-Television News Directors' Association (RTNDA) sat in rapt attention as Edward R. Murrow unburdened himself of the feelings that had begun damming up within him. Advance copies of the October 15, 1958 speech had been carefully circulated by Murrow to select people both in and out of CBS. William Paley did not receive a copy.

From the beginning of his career, Ed Murrow understood the educational power of radio and television. Lately, he could only stand by helplessly as news programming was shunted aside for profit-making network quiz and entertainment shows. Now, the quiz shows, which had taken the networks by storm, found themselves tainted by scandal. Criminal charges of fraud and answer-rigging were filed; the networks were disgraced. Murrow could no longer remain quiet. Depressed at the loss of *See It Now*, he gratefully accepted the invitation of the RTNDA to speak. For weeks, he had carefully crafted what he would say.

"This nation," he continued, "is in mortal danger. . . . Surely we shall pay for using this most powerful instrument of communication to insulate the citizenry from the hard and demanding realities which are to be faced if we are to survive." In a direct swipe at the manner in which his own network's executives had treated a vital news story, he said, "It is difficult to believe that this decision was made by men who love, respect, and understand news." He warned his colleagues they had a moral and professional obligation to halt the slide of television news away from serious journalism.

This instrument can teach, it can illuminate; yes, and it can even inspire. But it can do so only to the extent that humans are determined [to pursue] it to those ends. Otherwise, it is merely wires and lights in a box. There is a great and perhaps decisive battle to be fought against ignorance, intolerance, and indifference. This weapon of television could be useful.

The speech was widely acclaimed. But it did not satisfy Murrow. His depression deepened and his cigarette-induced coughing worsened. His favorite brand was Camel—no filters. He smoked four packs a day, on average. Casey recalls, "He'd get out of bed, slip those legs down onto the floor and light up." When Casey, still a child, accompanied his father to the CBS studios in New York, Ed sometimes sent him out to buy a carton of Camels. Even after five thousand broadcasts, he still found his work stressful. "I've got a watermelon in my belly every night," he told a reporter. "I guess there isn't a moment during the show when I don't have a cigarette in my hand."

He began not to feel well and his visits to physicians increased. Tests revealed nothing except that he needed a rest. Taking advantage of a clause in his contract, he requested a sabbatical—a year's leave of absence for the 1959–60 broadcast season. Janet was thrilled. "I'd never thought I'd see the day when he'd do it," she said. "Why," she continued, "we hadn't had any kind of social life at all, very little opportunity to see our friends."

On his last daily radio broadcast on June 26, 1959, Ed Murrow told his listeners about his plans for the forthcoming year.

Tonight this reporter departs the microphone for a year's leave of absence—a departure which has been rather over-publicized. . . . The next year will be spent in traveling, reading, listening, keeping silent. . . . Unless curiosity curdles, I shall return to face this frightening microphone with a little more knowledge and assurance, at least the illusion, that I know what I am talking about. . . .

On August 26, Ed, Janet, and Casey boarded a steamship for Europe and the beginning of an extended family tour around the world. Not that Ed would be completely idle; he left with plans to do special reports en route. Accompanying the family to Europe in the ship's hold was Ed's favorite automobile, a black Ford Thunderbird.

After a visit to the Scandinavian countries, Ed went on to Iran to interview the Shah while Janet took Casey to Switzerland to enroll him temporarily in a boarding school. She then met Ed in London where they visited with old friends. While in London, Murrow delivered a highly publicized speech on the role of television in politics. At the end of November, Ed and Janet drove the Thunderbird through the French countryside to pick up Casey and celebrate Christmas in Switzerland. Then, the reunited family drove into Italy and, on January 25, 1960, boarded the steamer *Theodor Herzl* in Naples for Israel. It was a rare opportunity for the family to spend extended time together. "The trip was fascinating," Casey later said, "in part because both of my parents were fairly relaxed—as relaxed as you can be when traveling."

To fourteen-year-old Casey, the visit to Israel was special. Their activities were reported in the country's newspapers. One Israeli journalist, watching Murrow filming a program, noticed that "Mr. Murrow wielded the familiar cigarette in his left hand." For most of their stay, Casey and Ed toured together in the black Thunderbird. Janet fell ill and spent most of her time in Israel resting at an inn in the Galilee. "We traveled all over the country," Casey recalled. "It was a great experience for me. He was always the reporter. He was always asking questions. He was just happy to kick around with me, so that was a pleasure."

When Ed Murrow interviewed General Moshe Dayan for a *Small World* broadcast, a *Jerusalem Post* reporter noted the following in a front-page story: "An unofficial assistant in the studio was Mr. Murrow's fourteen-year-old son, Casey."

Though Casey was a young teenager, Ed treated him as an adult traveling companion. It was not all relaxation and touring. For the second time during the sabbatical, Murrow broke his radio silence to report on a breaking news story. The first had been to tell listeners about the British election and now, in Israel, to provide background on the escalating violence on the Syrian border. Casey vividly recalled the trip they took with military escort to the Golan Heights on Israel's northern border, then under frequent shelling from Syrian artillery.

We went up to the Golan Heights and saw some Roman ruins. . . . There was a switchback road that went up to one of the border outposts. It was just an incredible ride with a guy who knew the road—he had to, or he would have killed us all.

I was very involved with binoculars at that time. I carried a pair of binoculars almost everywhere I went. One of the officers was showing us where the Syrian gun emplacements were, and I picked up my binoculars and he hit me just like that—really cut me across my nose to get the binoculars out—get the reflection away because he said they'd shoot at that instantly.

After Israel, the much-used Thunderbird was sent back to the United States while the family flew off to India and then to Hawaii. After a stop in Washington to visit their family, the Murrows returned home to New York on May 6, 1960, exhausted but fulfilled.

Shortly after their return from England at the end of World War II, the Murrows had settled into two distinct lives: the workaday world of the city, and the weekend-and-vacation retreat in the country. In 1950, the Murrows moved from a townhouse on East Seventy-fourth Street to a prestigious eleven-room apartment on Park Avenue. The apartment was more a child's playroom, with Casey's toys everywhere, than a decorator's dream home.

Ed had also bought a fourteen-acre property, with a sturdy log cabin included, seventy-five miles north of New York City at Quaker Hill in Pawling, New York. Quaker Hill was dominated by Lowell Thomas, the famous explorer and broadcaster, who years earlier had bought up much of the land in the area to create an exclusive neighborhood. Introduced to the rustic area and lifestyle by Thomas, Ed decided to buy property there. His log cabin was not a rough-hewn structure but a comfortable and well-built house which even had a maid's room. An immense stone fireplace welcomed visitors to the living room. For Murrow, it was the perfect place to unwind from the pressures of work.

Neighbors were rich and famous, including former New York Governor Thomas E. Dewey and author and minister Norman Vincent Peale. The Murrows were welcomed into the close-knit circle from the first. Although friendly with his neighbors, Ed was more interested in the area's hunting, fishing, and natural beauty. It was Casey who named their log cabin Rumblewood, since the name reminded him of the sound the winds made as they rustled through the attic eaves.

The financial success of *Person to Person* allowed Murrow to eventually trade Rumblewood for Glen Arden, a two-hundred-eighty-acre farm also in Quaker Hill. By 1955, Murrow was making a larger salary than the CBS founder and board chairman, William Paley. Glen Arden was a working farm, with cultivated land and sixty head of cattle. The day-to-day operations were left in the hands of a resident caretaker. Ed bought a large Caterpillar tractor. "We spent a lot of hours running that thing," Casey remembered. "We built three ponds with that on our property; I did a chunk of the work and he did, too. It was a lot of fun. He would happily spend a whole day on that bulldozer and know what he was doing. He taught me to use a whole lot of equipment that, in retrospect, I never knew how he knew how to run."

Weekdays were spent in New York, where Casey went to school. His parents did their best to assure Casey a normal life. "They really struggled not to make [Ed's fame] a big deal," Casey remembered, "they tried not to spoil me." Once, when Casey mentioned his father's fame to a school friend, his furious mother admonished him not to speak about it. Guests were always welcome to the Murrow home. Casey remembered meeting famous people from England and elsewhere "who I had read about or heard about and suddenly, there they were in our apartment." Casey also recalled that during the McCarthy period "when there were a lot of threats against them and against me, I never knew that was going on at the time. They worked so hard to keep things normal." Only later did Casey discover that his father had helped blacklisted writers and reporters with loans for their legal defenses.

But life was not normal. Janet had plans to fly off to visit friends when Ed told her of the upcoming McCarthy program. "Well," she told him, "in that case, I shouldn't go off to the Caribbean." "I don't know what difference it can make," Ed responded, "because I wouldn't be home much anyway."

She missed the broadcast. But when she landed in New York
the next day, Ed was there to meet her. His first words
alarmed her. "We must never allow Casey to be unattended."
For a long time thereafter, Casey was escorted daily by Janet
or the maid to and from school. "Those were difficult times,"
Fred Friendly recalled. "Ed always felt that there were times
during the McCarthy period when his phone was
bugged."

McCarthy's impact on the American scene declined quickly
after the *See It Now* broadcasts of 1954, but McCarthyism lin-
gered on. In 1955, Ed's routine request for a passport renewal
put him in exactly the type of situation he had reported about
others. The Passport Office would not issue the new passport
unless he signed a statement declaring that he was never a
Communist and had never belonged to any organization seeking the overthrow of the United States government. It
seemed that an anonymous source had charged Murrow with
disloyalty. Murrow was furious that his loyalty to the United
States had been questioned and refused to sign.

He went to Washington and met with an official of the
Passport Office. Murrow asked for the nature of the deroga-
tory information against him. The official replied that he
could not make that known. Murrow then asked if his file
"contained anonymous, casual information without proof or
substantiation." The official said it did, referring to a piece in
*Counterattack*, the rabidly anti-Communist newsletter which
was engaged in an ongoing attack on Murrow. The official
went on to say that although the information in the file was
not a serious problem, existing regulations required the
signed statement before the passport could be released.

Murrow signed, under protest. Even he was not immune from McCarthyism.

Ed struggled with the knowledge that he had not always been wealthy. His friends accused him of "boasting" about his underprivileged childhood. "It must have been very strange," Casey said about his father, "to have grown up in an environment without much money and then to have quite a lot. He liked that backwoods image. I'm not sure it was entirely true that the family was incredibly poor. They were poor by any of our standards today but they were not always at the bottom of the heap." Ed always chafed under the yoke of fame. Particularly after he became a television personality, it became almost impossible for him to blend into a crowd. People recognized him everywhere.

Life in the city tended to be uneventful and for Janet, perhaps a bit boring. Ed worked hard and long hours; by the time he got home, after 8:30 P.M., he was usually too tired to go out. "He brought his worries and concerns home with him and spent a lot of time on the telephone," Casey remembered. Janet and Ed would have a quiet dinner at about nine. Casey ate earlier and did not get much chance to see his father during the week.

When Casey was quite young, Ed involved him in annual holiday broadcasts. Casey remembers one Christmas show where "we went shopping for my mother with a sound crew. It was fun and made for a cute Christmassy broadcast, but I think he also recognized he was taking advantage of me." Indeed, Murrow later told a newspaper interviewer why he stopped including Casey in his broadcasts. "I think anything that sets a kid apart is no service to the kid."

As Casey grew older, his father took him along on assignments and to the studio. "That was fun," Casey recalled. "He was more than willing to include me but he never wanted me to take on a role of involvement or importance. If I wanted to hang around with the sound guys and the cameraman, that was what I wanted to do anyway."

Once a week friends might be invited to dinner. Usually, the guests were old acquaintances from Europe or from Murrow's life before radio. These were quiet, almost informal affairs, which gave Ed further opportunity to do what he liked best—talk to people and learn from them. It was his way of observing the world. No person was too unimportant; no event minor enough.

Former CBS correspondent Charles Kuralt likes to recall an incident from his youth when he first met the legendary Edward R. Murrow. Kuralt, then in high school and a writer for his school paper, was accompanying Murrow, who had just spoken at the school, back to the airport. Instead of discussing the world situation or life at CBS, Kuralt found himself answering Murrow's questions about the student newspaper and the condition of the local cotton crop. Kuralt later said, "I was too young and inexperienced to realize that I had spent an hour with a consummate reporter." Murrow, who faced "an hour with nothing more to dig into than the opinions of a couple of kids," proceeded to interview them on things they knew and cared about.

Weekends were for relaxing. "Our life," Janet said, "consisted of work and rest. Rest for more work!" Janet and Casey usually drove up to Quaker Hill on Friday afternoons and Ed joined them the next day after doing the weekly *Person to Person* show on Friday evenings at 10:30. "He relaxed," Janet said, "by playing golf, and by conversing—telling stories—with friends and drinking a bit. But it was getting together with friends."

He and Casey went shooting—Ed always had a gun; Janet joined them for golf. "I didn't shoot," Janet explained. "I felt it was too hard on my shoulder." Casey later admitted he never liked golf but played only because he enjoyed his father's company. Their life at Quaker Hill was a family affair. "That was a wonderful environment for me," Casey fondly recalled, "and that is where I saw the most of my father. My strongest associations with him in a relaxed environment were there, and not in the city at all."

During summer vacations, Murrow sometimes broadcast from a specially built studio in Lowell Thomas's nearby home in Pawling. Ed was a poor speller and grammarian but typed his own commentary pieces. Young Casey enjoyed reading these scripts because "my teachers in school said I had to do it just this certain way and he didn't do it that way. I thought that was great. The punctuation was his own invention to give him clues for pauses. It was his code and I never understood it."

Roscoe Murrow had suffered a crippling stroke in 1947, from which he never fully recovered. Ethel, without complaint, tended to his needs until he died in 1955. Proud and fiercely independent, Ethel turned to her sons for help only when absolutely necessary. "She put up with a lot of worry," Janet fondly remembered with a bit of understatement, "and did it very well!" When an insurance company sent her a letter that she didn't understand, she forwarded it to Ed. To conserve paper, she typed her typically unassuming remarks to her son in the blank space on the bottom of the letter. "Ed

Dear—I know full well how busy you are, also how tired you must be, but will you please examine the papers. . . ." He took care of the major and minor crises, paid medical bills, and set up a trust fund for his mother.

Most important to Ethel were the prolonged summer family visits to Washington State. Usually, Janet and Casey traveled out first and Ed joined them later. Ethel enjoyed collecting antiques, always driving a hard bargain with store owners as she led the younger Murrows from one shop to another. Casey remembers one particular incident when he, Ethel, and Ed went into a small antique store in Vancouver, British Columbia. She picked out "a clock that wouldn't work but she knew was really special." She then proceeded to bargain with the owner to drive the price down. Casey looked on with embarrassment as the "owner said to my dad he would be happy to sell him the clock if he would just leave!"

The clock saga did not end there. When the store owner visited Ethel to adjust the clock, he saw that she had put it in a doorway. She would not move it. The store owner, concerned about Ethel's safety because he thought the clock could topple over, wrote to Ed, who could only respond, "I'm afraid there is very little either one of us could do about the position of the clock, as you have undoubtedly gathered. My mother is a very opinionated person and she has visualized the clock in that position since she first saw it. I shall try to persuade her gently by letter, but I have little hope of success."

The sabbatical year abroad quickly faded into a dreamy memory as Ed now faced the harshest years of his life. His health was slowly deteriorating, but what mattered most to him was his diminishing role at CBS. Although his radio programs continued, *See It Now* was history and his television role was limited. Now it was 1960, a presidential year, and broadcasting-legend Murrow found himself on convention floors with younger reporters. The physical demands took a toll on him, but he did not complain. He only knew he could not continue this way. John F. Kennedy, the newly elected president of the United States, offered Murrow a way out.

*Murrow shaking hands with John F. Kennedy, 1961 (WSU)*

# CHAPTER TEN

# The Bureaucrat

*Under Murrow, we have told the truth.*
　　　　　　—Arthur Schlesinger, Jr.

$\text{T}$he United States Information Agency (USIA) was established in 1953 to promote American culture, life, and politics abroad. Now its network of libraries and information centers spans over a hundred countries around the world. Millions of listeners tune in daily to its popular shortwave radio service, the Voice of America. The agency produces television programs, films, pamphlets, exhibits, and books. It sponsors student exchanges, seminars, and cultural activities. The USIA also monitors international public opinion of United States policies.

To some during the Cold War, the USIA served merely a propaganda function. Much of the USIA's efforts during the 1950s focused on the Communist world and the emerging countries where Communism and democracy competed for the hearts and minds of millions. Ed Murrow realized that the services provided by the USIA existed for more universal purposes. "We seek to convince," he said late in 1961, "that the goal we seek is a guide for enrichment and not a guise for enslavement."

Ed Murrow accepted President John F. Kennedy's invitation to become director of the United States Information Agency. He did so, said his USIA deputy, Donald M. Wilson, "because he had really reached the end of the road at CBS. . . . He was a famous man who had no forum and he needed a new career." Murrow entered the new administration with no particular loyalty to Kennedy. Casey Murrow felt his father "thought it was a real privilege to take this job. He knew he wasn't going to be very visible or make as much money as he had at CBS. But it was a neat opportunity to serve the country in a realm that he really did know something about." Indeed, by taking the job, he reduced his yearly salary from two hundred thousand dollars to twenty thousand. Before accepting the position, Ed insisted that he be involved in decision-making at the highest levels of government. The president made him a nonvoting member of the National Security Council and invited his participation in Cabinet meetings.

Ed always had appreciated the power of news to sway foreign opinion about America. In 1953, at the height of Senator McCarthy's popularity, Murrow testified before a Senate subcommittee about the Voice of America. Without realizing it at the time, he described the principles that would later guide him as head of the USIA. "We have no choice," he said, "but to try to tell the truth about ourselves." He saw a role for the USIA that went beyond the limitations of propaganda.

I do not believe that we can or should slant or angle the news broadcasts from this country. We are not a controlled society.

There are too many alternate sources of information in the Western world to permit the successful slanting of news. We should, above everything else, attempt to achieve credibility, for the measure of our success will be the degree to which we are believed.

In March 1961, Murrow appeared before the Senate Foreign Relations Committee to repeat his view during his confirmation hearing.

We shall operate on the basis of truth . . . we shall constantly reiterate our faith in freedom. We cannot imitate the tactics or the techniques of the dictatorships that now ride the backs of most of this planet's people. We cannot threaten, we must persuade. Freedom cannot be imposed, it must be sought for, and frequently fought for.

On January 31, 1961, Murrow said farewell to CBS employees and affiliated stations around the country over closed-circuit television. "Some part of my heart will stay with CBS," he told his colleagues. Some noticed the tinge of emotion in his voice as he ended his talk with "I wish you all good luck and good night." Network officials threw a lavish party in his honor. The break was final. Ed Murrow was on his way to Washington, D.C.

His appointment process took a long time. The FBI conducted an exhaustive investigation of his past. Every crank letter in his file was examined. Some in Washington could not forgive Murrow's continual insistence on speaking out on politically unpopular issues. Conservative groups flooded Washington with letters opposing him. One Texas minister wrote, "This is a strategic spot to which you have appointed Mr. Murrow. Infiltration is one of the Communists' most effective weapons." In the end, Edward R. Murrow's nomination was unanimously confirmed by the United States Senate.

Ed and Janet sold their apartment on Park Avenue in New York and bought a house in Washington. Although the Kennedy presidency brought with it an unending rush of social activities, the Murrows kept mainly to themselves and their circle of friends. There were occasional private dinners at the White House. During one dinner in 1962 with the Kennedys and the Wilsons, the president asked Ed if he would consider running for the United States Senate from New York. "It was one of the few times I've seen Ed totally at a loss for words," Don Wilson, deputy director of the USIA, remembered. "I'd make a terrible candidate," Murrow told the president.

If Ed thought he was exchanging his pressure-filled CBS days for a life of ordered routine and more time with his family, he quickly discovered the truth. Don Wilson met the Murrows at the train station with a pile of thick briefing books, documents, and reports. That was only the beginning. Casey described his father as "overwhelmed by how complicated a system it was."

The 1960s was a period of intense unrest in many countries that were once colonies of Western democracies. It was no surprise that many revolutionaries were supported by the Soviet Union and were Communist inspired. The United States countered with massive amounts of foreign and military aid. The role of the USIA assumed greater importance in the growing world struggle between Communism and democracy. Ed Murrow did not have an easy job.

Time with Casey had always been limited, so it was with pride that Ed, off to give a July speech in Seattle, Washington, wrote President Kennedy, "I am planning to leave for the West Coast (traveling by Thunderbird with Casey as co-pilot)." Ed promised to file reports with the president "as to what folks in the gas stations and motels think of your foreign policy."

Casey had just received his driver's license and Ed allowed him to do most of the driving. They made frequent stops to talk with "truck drivers, motel operators, farm equipment salesmen, farmers, service station operators" for "a personal unscientific poll by a one-time reporter." Writing to Kennedy from the Rocket Motel, Joplin, Missouri, Ed related the opinions of such diverse Americans as poet Carl Sandburg, a woman selling cider in Tennessee, and a senior citizen in Roaring Gap, North Carolina. The trip ended abruptly in Salt Lake City when Ed was summoned back to Washington on official business.

That Christmas, the Murrow family gathered in Arizona for a long-overdue reunion. Ed and his brothers even convinced Ethel to come by airplane—her first such trip. Although her health was failing, Ethel enjoyed the visit. Ed and Casey then accompanied her home by plane and returned to Washington. Within a few days, Ed received the news that his mother had died.

Ed Murrow was a superb and insightful reporter. He was not a politician. That was clearly evident in an embarrassing incident that occurred shortly after his joining the USIA. The

British Broadcasting Corporation had arranged with CBS to air Murrow's *Harvest of Shame* program about American migrant workers. The Kennedy administration worried that the highly acclaimed documentary would give British viewers an uncomplimentary view of America. Murrow, who had written and reported the program while at CBS, telephoned the BBC in his new role as USIA director, to request the cancellation of his own program. The resulting publicity unleashed a storm of protest about censorship from Ed's longtime supporters and friends. A chagrined Murrow apologized, admitting he had been "both foolish and futile" in trying to cancel the program.

The political nature of his job, however, could not be ignored. As a governmental agency, the USIA depended on the goodwill, and votes, of Congress for funds. The buck stopped on Capitol Hill in the person of Congressman John J. Rooney of Brooklyn, New York, who chaired the subcommittee charged with appropriating funds to the USIA. Murrow always prided himself on his ability to reason with others on a variety of issues. He never fully succeeded with Rooney. Each trip to Capitol Hill and Rooney's subcommittee was a demeaning exercise. During a 1963 speech, Ed decried the latest attempts to cut his agency's already meager budget. "We are being outspent, outpublished, and outbroadcast," Murrow said. "We are a first-rate power. We must speak with a first-rate voice abroad."

"He didn't like the way USIA was used as a political football," Casey later commented. "He didn't like being insulted when he went up there to argue for his budget. He certainly played a fair amount of hardball with Congress once he found out that that's the way certain ones wanted to treat him." As

Murrow's health began to worsen, those trips became nearly unbearable for the proud director.

Ed Murrow's personal commitment and philosophy brought a new sense of mission to the USIA and improved morale among employees. One of his first acts was to publicly reinstate Reed Harris to the agency as executive assistant to the director. Harris, featured on Murrow's 1954 *See It Now* program about Senator McCarthy, had lost his job eight years earlier. Others, dismissed during the McCarthy era, returned to the agency.

Murrow's high visibility as the best-known Kennedy appointee also did not hurt the agency's public image. The USIA had rarely been visible in previous administrations. Murrow, through his supportive management style, shaped the USIA into an independent and respected agency. Historian Arthur Schlesinger said that Murrow "revitalized the USIA, imbued it with his own bravery and honesty and directed its efforts especially in the developing nations." His years as a reporter trained him to listen and analyze well. He spoke only infrequently at National Security Council meetings. But when he spoke, everyone listened. His colleagues learned to respect his educated insight on diplomacy and world affairs.

Yet, the president's promise to make Murrow part of the government's decision-making process was forgotten in the early days of the new administration. In 1960, the island of Cuba, just ninety miles from the United States, became the first Western Hemisphere country to declare itself Communist. The previous administration had supported Cuban exile attempts to overthrow the regime of Fidel Castro forcibly. Even before Kennedy took the oath of office, plans were in place for a United States–supported invasion of Cuba by armed Cuban exiles. On the morning of April 17, 1961, approximately fourteen hundred armed men went ashore at the Bay of Pigs in Cuba. To their surprise, they were instantly pinned down. Everything went wrong and without supplies and expected air cover, the invasion ended within three days; 114 exiles were killed and another 1,189 taken prisoner. It was a military and political disaster for the fledgling Kennedy administration.

Murrow first heard of the Bay of Pigs plan just a few days before the invasion from his deputy, Don Wilson, who learned of the plan from a *New York Times* reporter. Murrow, realizing it was too late to voice his objections, was privately furious with the White House but remained quiet publicly. When the dust settled, President Kennedy realized his error in not involving Murrow. According to Wilson, "From that time on, Murrow was well on his way to being trusted and much more brought into confidences at the White House." This marked the beginning of a real role for the USIA in determining foreign policy. Other crises followed, but thanks to Murrow, never again was the USIA left out of the decision-making loop.

Murrow returned to the twelve-hour, seven-day-a-week work schedule he had favored while at CBS. At home, there were always briefing books to study and reports to digest. There were trips abroad to visit USIA libraries and outposts in Europe, South America, the Middle East, and West Africa. He was in Berlin in 1961 and witnessed construction of the Berlin Wall by the Communists to isolate their half of the city from Western influences. Outraged, he successfully urged the Kennedy administration to use pictures extensively so the world could see what the Communists were doing.

When the administration debated how to deal with the Soviet threat to resume nuclear testing, Murrow's advice prevailed at the White House and proved a diplomatic victory for the United States. "We can't go right away," Murrow said. "We've got to wait and let the full impact of the Russian testing sink in on people. Let ourselves be forced to test."

Murrow provided the White House with a continual flow of overseas opinion polls and recommendations for presidential action. Ed's underlying strategy was summarized in a memorandum he wrote to the president in February 1961: "USIA programs are more convincing abroad if they reflect convictions we hold at home. USIA programs are more appealing abroad if they utilize the finest talents we have in our country." He spoke before entertainment, publishing, and film groups on ways to promote American culture abroad.

When the president's popular Peace Corps—young American volunteers in developing countries—met with derision from the Soviet Union, Murrow had a recommendation for Kennedy. "At your next news conference, you should say in answer to a question that you would be delighted to see Russians working alongside Americans and others in an effort to improve health, education, and public services in the emerging countries."

In the fall of 1962, Murrow took ill while in Teheran, Iran. The diagnosis was pleurisy, an inflammation of the lungs. He was sent back to Washington. Janet urged him to enter a hospital, but he insisted on returning to Pawling, New York, for a rest. The rest did not help and he reluctantly returned to Washington on October 12 to enter the Bethesda Naval Hospital. Doctors examined him and took X rays; their diagnosis was pneumonia. Reading the X rays, they took notice of a small shadow on a lung but decided it was just scar tissue.

While Murrow lay bedridden at Bethesda, the greatest crisis of John Kennedy's presidency unfolded nearby behind closed doors. The Cuban Missile Crisis brought the world close to nuclear war between the United States and the Soviet Union. While the world hovered on the edge of self-destruction, Ed Murrow lay helpless in bed. His deputy, Don Wilson, represented the agency well during the crisis, but Murrow later said that was "the most frustrating experience of my life."

A month later, he was back at work, but without his earlier vigor. This was the beginning of a series of worsening illnesses for Ed. He continued to smoke cigarettes heavily while seeing doctors more frequently. The doctors kept writing prescriptions and his collection of pill bottles grew. During his first year and a half at USIA, Ed, never plump, noticeably lost weight. Others became aware of his nearly continuous coughing and a simultaneous increase in his consumption of alcoholic drinks.

In September 1963, while giving a speech in Philadelphia, he noticed a change in his voice. "Propaganda is far more what we do than what we say," he told his listeners. "We will be known far more by what we are than by what we say or do." Suddenly, the familiar baritone sound turned raspy and there was a pain in his throat. He returned to Washington, where doctors discovered lung cancer. They operated on October 6 and removed his diseased left lung, the same lung on which a spot had been detected and apparently misdiagnosed a year earlier. In an act of decided willfulness, Ed Murrow chose that moment to stop smoking. "It was absolutely horrible for him," Casey remembered. "Clearly, he went through a withdrawal process." Never again did he light up a cigarette. But it was too late to stop the damage to his body. "He used to say," Casey added, "he hoped there would be a cure before he got cancer."

Six weeks later, stunned by the assassination of John F. Kennedy, a weakened Murrow mustered his strength to leave his bed and travel to the White House to pay his last respects to the fallen president. Ed was not happy with Lyndon Johnson. Aside from his personal health concerns, Ed knew he could not work with the new president, and he decided to resign. Johnson, used to getting his own way, would not consider any resignations from his new administration without a replacement ready to take over. He did not want anyone to associate resignation with dissatisfaction.

"I deem it my duty to ask you to accept my resignation," Murrow wrote President Johnson on December 19, 1963. "I would be grateful if you could arrange to relieve me of my duties by mid-January." He even met with Johnson to press the point. There was no immediate response from the White House. "Dad felt it was very irresponsible," Casey recalled, "because there ought to be some good person to head the Agency. He [Murrow] wasn't that person at the time."

Meanwhile, Ed and Janet made plans to travel to California for a sun-drenched rest in a seaside rental home arranged by Dr. Jonas Salk. As they were about to board the plane, the president reached Ed by telephone at Dulles Airport to say he finally had a replacement for him. Less than three years after entering government service, Ed Murrow was again a private person. In a gracious acceptance letter, President Johnson told Murrow, "It is with the greatest reluctance that I yield to your insistence and accept your resignation. You leave," he added, "with the thanks of a grateful President and a grateful nation."

By June 1964, the Murrows were back at Quaker Hill in Pawling, New York. A steady stream of guests visited to offer encouragement. Feeling stronger, Ed participated in a nostalgic CBS News program to mark the closing of Studio 9 and the move to new network facilities on New York's West Fifty-seventh Street. It was Murrow's last broadcast. In September, Ed went to Washington, where President Johnson presented him with the Medal of Freedom, the highest civilian honor bestowed on a citizen by the United States. Shortly thereafter, Queen Elizabeth II honored Murrow's love of England by bestowing on him the title of Honorary Knight Commander of the Most Excellent Order of the British Empire.

A few months later, Murrow was in a New York hospital, where a malignant tumor was removed from near his brain. After his release from the hospital, he and Janet moved into a Manhattan apartment as he underwent radiation therapy to halt the progression of the cancer. But it was too late. Despite the radiation treatments, the cancer spread to his brain. He was readmitted to the hospital.

He understood the seriousness of his condition and wanted to die in the familiar, comfortable environs of Quaker Hill. Janet had him moved home, where nurses attended to his needs around the clock. She was in constant attendance. Casey, then a freshman at Yale University, came home on weekends. Toward the end of his life, Ed Murrow displayed the open affection to his wife and son that he had rarely shown when he was healthy. Casey sadly recalled, "The last few years were rough for him in so many ways but obviously physically, if not emotionally. He had never really suffered in that way previously. I don't think he knew how to reach out to friends or family either—or didn't want to." He died, as Janet sat by his bedside, on April 27, 1965, two days after his fifty-seventh birthday.

*Murrow portrait (National Archives)*

# Good Night and Good Luck

*No one will ever be able to fill the unique place Ed Murrow held in broadcasting.*
                —William Paley

Ida Lou Anderson would have been proud of her favorite student. Edward R. Murrow had not only become a technical master of the spoken word, but the conscience and voice of his generation. He had learned his lessons well: from his mother, compassion, morality, and faith; and from his teachers, the power of knowledge and clear thinking. From them he inherited the courage to confront fear and evil. CBS News correspondent Eric Sevareid eloquently said of his colleague, "The poetry of America was in his bones. . . . He was a shooting star and we will live in his after-glow a very long time."

The nationally broadcast dedication ceremony of the United States Holocaust Memorial Museum in Washington, D.C., in April 1993 featured a reading of Ed Murrow's "Report from Buchenwald." Six years earlier, the Holocaust Council had presented its coveted Eisenhower Liberation Medal in Murrow's memory. *CBS Evening News* anchor Dan Rather, asked to read from Murrow's Buchenwald report, instead played a tape. He wanted the audience to "hear it from Murrow himself, crackling through the wire, the way it was then." Janet Murrow, accepting on behalf of her late husband, told the audience, "He always felt so strongly that we all must work to prevent persecution and injustice."

Murrow died in 1965: he has not been forgotten. Important professional awards have been established in his memory; a high school in New York City proudly bears his name. He is quoted, referred to, and thought of whenever the question of broadcast-news excellence is raised.

In early 1994, the United States Postal Service issued a commemorative stamp in his honor. A few months earlier, at the annual convention of the Radio and Television News Directors Association in the fall of 1993, Dan Rather delivered a speech in which he paid a poignant tribute to Murrow.

He was the best reporter of his generation. The best reporter in broadcasting or print. He reported, he led, he made the best broadcasts of his time, both in radio and television. And those broadcasts remain, to this day, the best of all time. They include the *This . . . Is London* broadcasts from the Battle of Britain, the radio report from the death camp at Buchenwald, and the television programs on Joseph McCarthy, and *Harvest of Shame.*

Ed Murrow was not only the founding saint of broadcast news and the best-ever practitioner of it, he also set standards for excellence and courage that remain the standards, the world over. And, along the way, he made the best speech ever by anyone in our business.

He was, in short, a hero. No wonder they have issued a stamp in his name.

Then, in remarks reminiscent of Murrow's words before the same group in 1958, Rather restated many of the same charges against the broadcast industry Murrow had made thirty-five years earlier. He decried the increasing reliance on sensationalism and "glitz" to boost ratings and sell advertising time. Then, as Murrow had done, Rather challenged his colleagues to "practice the idealism" that attracted them to their profession in the first place.

Shortly after Murrow's death, each of the major radio and television networks, NBC, ABC, and CBS, aired programs in Murrow's honor. The best-known names in broadcast journalism spoke of their personal and professional loss. Many, hired or influenced by Murrow himself, were the living legacies of the great broadcast legend. "Everything that you see in broadcasting journalism that is any good," Charles Collingwood of CBS said, "owes something to Ed Murrow. Murrow had absolute courage . . . absolute integrity." Robert Trout eulogized his longtime colleague by saying, "There is no way to say farewell to him for those of us who work in the field. Everyday we use tools and techniques that he made."

The life of Edward R. Murrow was dedicated to education in its broadest sense, and to people, particularly young people. Former CBS correspondent Charles Kuralt fondly remembers the impact Murrow had on him.

I always had the feeling he was interested in my work long before it could have been called in any way promising. This was impressive in one who towered above the crowd of broadcast journalists as he did, and who had so much on his mind. His attitude toward the young I have tried to keep in mind as I've grown older. Beginners need confidence, of course. I never had the nerve to ask Murrow for advice directly, but if I had, I believe he would have said, "Become good at what you do, and everything else will take care of itself."

# Bibliography

There are three definitive biographies of Edward R. Murrow.

Kendrick, Alexander. *Prime Time: The Life of Edward R. Murrow.* Boston: Little, Brown, 1969.

Persico, Joseph. *Edward R. Murrow, American Original.* New York: McGraw-Hill, 1988.

Sperber, A. M. *Murrow: His Life and Times.* New York: Freundlich, 1986.

Several books contain selections from Murrow's radio and television broadcasts.

Bliss, Edward J., ed. *In Search of Light: The Broadcasts of Edward R. Murrow.* New York: Alfred A. Knopf, 1967.

Murrow, Edward R. *This Is London*. New York: Simon and Schuster, 1941.

Murrow, Edward R. and Fred W. Friendly, eds. *See It Now: A Selection in Text and Pictures*. New York: Simon and Schuster, 1955.

Other books provide useful background information about the development of radio news.

Barnouw, Erik A. *A History of Broadcasting in the United States* (3 vols.). New York: Oxford University Press, 1970.

Bliss, Edward J. *Now the News*. New York: Columbia University Press, 1991.

Finkelstein, Norman H. *Sounds in the Air: The Golden Age of Radio*. New York: Scribners, 1993.

Friendly, Fred W. *Due to Circumstances Beyond Our Control*. New York: Random House, 1967.

Kuralt, Charles. *A Life on the Road*. New York: Putnam, 1990.

# Research Notes

The largest number of documents relating to the career of Edward R. Murrow may be found in the Murrow Collection at the Fletcher School of Law and Diplomacy, Tufts University, Medford, Massachusetts. Located here are Murrow's professional correspondence, program scripts, family information, and related files.

Two documents in particular provide an intimate glimpse of Edward R. Murrow as a young man. The first is an unpublished typescript of a tribute program presented by the General Aid Committee of the church attended by Ethel and Roscoe Murrow in Bellingham, Washington. Although it is undated, "Those Murrow Boys" was probably written in 1941 or 1942. The second, "To Casey Murrow: Memories of Your Father," was written in 1965 by Murrow's friend Chester Williams. It contains interesting glimpses of Murrow during his NSFA and IIE days.

The Manuscript, Archives, and Special Collections of Washington State University, Pullman, Washington, contain yearbooks, school newspapers, and alumni materials related to Murrow's college years, including his special relationship with Ida Lou Anderson.

An article by Charles Kuralt, a native North Carolinian as was Murrow, provides a colleague's-eye view of Murrow. "Edward R. Murrow" appeared in the *North Carolina Historical Review*, Vol. XLVIII, No. 2, April 1971.

The CBS News Reference Library in New York contains official press releases, biographies, and clippings related to Murrow's career with the network.

Correspondence, press clippings, and reports from his years as director of the United States Information Agency may be found at the John F. Kennedy Presidential Library in Boston.

Visitors to New York City will find audio and video recordings of many Murrow broadcasts at the Museum of Television and Radio. A four-videotape set called *The Edward R. Murrow Television Collection*, produced by CBS News, is available at many public libraries and video stores.

# Index

*Page numbers in ialics refer to photos*

ABC (American Broadcasting
   Company), 163
Adams, Cedric, 127
African Americans, 37-39
American Civil Liberties Union, 2,
   10, 13, 124-25
*American School of the Air*, 46, 58
Anderson, Ida Lou, 31-32, 35, 46, 66,
   77, *81,* 161
Anderson, Marian, *94*
Armstrong, Louis, 121
*As Others See Us,* 113
Austria, German takeover of, 56-
   58

Barnouw, Erik, 101
Bate, Fred, 50
BBC, 54-55, 71, 104, 113, 152
Ben-Gurion, David, *96,* 129
Blacklisting, 4, 7, 139
Bloedell-Donovan Company, 25
Book banning, 7

Brewster, Janet Huntington. *See*
   Murrow, Janet
Britain. *See* England in World War II
British-American Liaison Board, 110
British Broadcasting Corporation.
   *See* BBC
Broadcast journalism, 12, 17, 43-44,
   50, 59-61, 75-78, 101-2, 110, 128-
   29, 131, 133-34, 148-49, 163
Bundles for Britain, 75, 77, 109
Burdett, Winston, 60

Campanella, Roy, 128
Campbell, Kay, 106
Campbell Soup Company, 114
CBS. *See also* Paley, William; *see also
   under* Murrow, Edward R.
  honors Murrow posthumously, xi-
    xii, 163
  logos of, 1, 76
  radio programming, 37, 43, 46-50,
    54-67, 108-9, 113-14, 126, 144

CBS (*continued*)
supports Murrow against
McCarthy, 16, 125
tape recorders forbidden by, 110
television programming, 1, 117-21,
126, 128-29, 130-31, 145
CBS Broadcast Center, xi, 158
*CBS Reports,* 130
Chamberlain, Neville, 62, 65, 69
China, 3, 40, 129
Churchill, Winston, 69, 115
Clooney, Rosemary, 128
Cold War, 2, 129, 147
Collingwood, Charles, 112, 163
Columbia Broadcasting System. *See*
CBS
Columbia University Teachers
College, 40
Committee in Aid of Displaced
German Scholars, 44-45
Communism and Communists, 3-
16, 121-25, 129, 147-48, 150-51,
153
Copland, Aaron, 130
Council on Foreign Relations, 46
Crosby, John, 12
Cuba, 153-54, 156
Czechoslovakia and Munich Pact,
61-62

Dayan, Moshe, 136
Dewey, Thomas E., 138
Downs, Bill, 60
Duggan, Stephen Pierce, 40-41, 44-
47

Edward VIII, king of England, 53
*Edward R. Murrow with the News,* 114

Eisenhower, Dwight D., 3, 7, 108,
129
Elizabeth II, queen of England, 158
England in World War II
Battle of Britain, 69-70, 74, 102-3,
162
bombing of London, 70-75, 106,
109
children evacuated from London,
67
class-consciousness, 66-67
declares war on Germany, 65
evacuation from Dunkirk, 68-69
Munich Pact, 61-62
Murrow broadcasts about, 66-67,
102, 162
Murrows' London apartment, 54,
74-75
En-lai, Chou, 129

Federal Communications
Commission, 48
Flanders, Ralph W., 8
Frankfurter, Felix, 104
Friendly, Fred W., 1, *98, 116,* 117-24,
130

Georgia
Atlanta NSFA convention, *37-39*
Germany. *See also* World War II
anti-Semitism in, 44-45
Berlin, *97, 100,* 105-7, 154
Buchenwald concentration camp,
111-12, 161-62
professors and exchange students
from, 44-45, 47-48
"Watch on the Ruhr" program, 129
and World War I, *53*
Glen Arden Farm, *90,* 138-39

Gould, Jack, 12
Graziano, Rocky, 128
Great Britain. *See* England in World
    War II
Great Depression, 35, 37, 40, 43, 45

Harris, Reed, 10, 153
*Hear It Now,* 117
Hitler, Adolph, 44-45, 53, 56, 58-62
Holocaust, 102-3, 111-12, 161-62
Holocaust Council, 161
Holocaust Memorial Museum, 161
Hottelet, Richard C., 60
House Un-American Activities
    Committee, 3

*I Can Hear It Now,* 117
Institute of International Education
    (IIE), 40-48
Internal Security Act, 4
Israel, *96, 129,* 136-37

Jackson, Mahalia, 128
Jewish Joint Distribution
    Committee, 44
Jews and anti-Semitism, 44-45, 48,
    58. *See also* Holocaust
Johnson, Lyndon B., 157-58
Jordan, Max, 50

Kaltenborn, H. V., 61-62
Keller, Helen, 12
Kendrick, Alexander, 102
Kennedy, John F., 128, 145, *146,* 148,
    150, 153-55, 157
Klauber, Ed., 49-50
Korean War, *85, 99,* 118-20, 125
Kuralt, Charles, 128, 142, 163-64

Lamb, George Van Buren, 20
Laski, Harold, 15-16
Lehan, Ed., 29-31
Lewis, Fulton, Jr., 13

McCarran Act, 4
McCarthy, Joseph, *xvi,* 1-2, 4-17, *87,*
    121-22, 125, 139-41, 148, 153, 162
MacLeish, Archibald, 77-78
Marx, Groucho, 128
Masaryk, Jan, 62
Matthews, Betty, 54, 56
Migrant workers, 130-31
Monroe, Marilyn, 128
Moses, Grandma, 121
Moss, Annie Lee, 14, 125
Mount Holyoke College, 41, 45
Munich crisis, 61-63
Murrow, Casey (son), 19, *84, 90,* 127,
    *132,* 134-35, 138-44, 151-52, 158-59
  birth of, 113
  on world tour with family, 135-37
  and father's USIA job, 148, 150,
    157
Murrow, Dewey (brother), 20-26, 30,
    151
Murrow, Edward R., *x,* 28, 42, 52, 64,
    *82-86, 88-100, 131, 160.*
  and Anderson, Ida Lou (speech
    teacher), 31-32, 35, 46, 66, 77, 161
  as Association of American
    Correspondents in London presi-
    dent, 110
  awards and honors, xi-xii, 35, 77-78,
    110, 113, 115, 158, 161-63
  bad with spelling and grammar, 22,
    143
  BBC offers top job to, 104
  birth of, 19

Murrow, Edward R. (*continued*)
  broadcasting philosophy and style
    of, xii-xiii, 2, 11, 32, 48, 55, 59-61,
    66-67, 78, 101-2, 104, 114-15, 119-
    20, 127-34, 148-49, 161-64
  and Buchenwald concentration
    camp, 111-12, 161-62
  and CBS, 1-2, 15-16, 37, 46-48, 144-
    45, 149, 158, 163
  on CBS board of directors, 115
  as CBS director of talks, 47-50
  as CBS European director, 49-113
  as CBS radio news anchor, 114-15,
    121, 126, 130, 135
  as CBS vice president, 113-14
  childhood of, *18*, 19-25
  and Committee in Aid of Displaced
    German Scholars, 44-45
  on Council on Foreign Relations, 46
  country home of, 138-39, 142-43
  covers 1960 political conventions,
    145
  death of, 159
  and debating, 22, 24, 31-32, 34
  dresses well, *33*, 54-55
  and drinking, 26, 30, 143
  education of, 22-26, 29-35, 40, 45,
    80
  in Europe with CBS, 49-113
  in Europe with IIE, 47
  in Europe with NSFA, 36, 39
  fame of, *63*, 76-77, 101, 126, 139-41
  flies on bombers, 105-8
  in forest fire, *33*
  and Friendly, Fred, 1, *98, 116*, 117-
    24, 130
  health of, *33*, 71, 104, 128, 134-35,
    144, 153, 155-59
  history interesting to, 20

  and Holocaust, 102-3, 111-12, 161-
    62
  influences public opinion during
    World War II, 75-78, 101-2
  and Institute of International
    Education, 40-48
  interviews: Adams, Cedric, 127;
    Armstrong, Louis, 121; Clooney,
    Rosemary, 128; Dayan, Moshe,
    136; En-lai, Chou, 129; Graziano,
    Rocky, 128; Jackson, Mahalia, 128;
    Kennedy, John F., 128; Marx,
    Groucho, 128; Monroe, Marilyn,
    128; Moses, Grandma, 121; Salk,
    Jonas, 121; Sandburg, Carl, 121,
    151; Shah of Iran, 136; Sinatra,
    Frank, 128; Stowkowski,
    Leopold, 128; Truman, Harry,
    129; Zorach, William, 127
  and Israel, *96*, 129, 136-37
  and Johnson, Lyndon B., 157-58
  in Kappa Sigma fraternity, 30, 32-33
  and Kennedy, John F., 128, 145, *146*,
    148, 150, 153-55, 157
  and Korean War, *85, 99*, 118-20, 125
  lifestyle of, 126, 137-44, 150
  marries Janet Brewster, 45-46
  and McCarthy, Joseph, 1-2, 8-17,
    121-22, 125, 139-41, 148, 162
  and migrant workers, 130-31
  and money, 23, 25-26, 40, 54, 138,
    141, 144, 148
  and "Murrow's Boys," 60, 108, 112
  on National Security Council, 148,
    153
  and National Student Federation of
    America, 34-41
  nicknames for, 19, 30
  in North Africa, 103-4

and outdoors, 19-20, 23, 25-26, 77, 138-39, 143

and Paley, William, 2, 49-50, 63, 77, 101, 105, 113-14, 133, 138-39

and Pearl Harbor story, 78-79

and Phi Beta Kappa, 35

and politics, 33-34, 38, 129, 150-52

and profanity, 26

programs: *American School of the Air*, 46, 58; *As Others See Us*, 113; *CBS Reports*, 130; *Edward R. Murrow with the News*, 114; "Harvest of Shame," 130-31, 152, 162; *I Can Hear It Now*, 117; "Orchestrated Hell," 106-8; *Person to Person*, 126-29, 142; *See It Now*, 1-2, 86, 117-26, 128-30, 134, 145; *Small World*, 130, 136; *This I Believe*, 126; *This . . . Is London*, 66-76, 102, 162; *University of the Air*, 37; *You Are There*, 113

punctuation system of, 143

and race discrimination, 37-39

radio course taken by, 34

radio debut of, 37

radio work with IIE, 41, 46, 49-50

radio work with NSFA, 37, 46, 50

relationship with brothers, 20-26, 30, 32

relationship with parents, 23, 143-44

and Roosevelt, Franklin D., 78-79, 102

in ROTC, 30, 33-34

and smoking, 26, 30, 126, 128, 134-36, 156-57

son (Casey) born to, 113

and Soviet Union, 13, 16, 40

tape-records paratroopers, 110

television debut of, 117-18

trademark lines of, 62, 76-77

and Truman, Harry, 89, 129

unhappy in broadcasting, 129-30, 133-35

as U.S. Information Agency director, 147-58

at Washington State University, 26, 28, 29-35

works as school bus driver, 24-25

works as ship's social director, 47

works for lumber company, 24-26, 29-30, 32-33, 40

works in railroad yards, 29

works in sorority house, 29

on world tour with family, 135-37

World War II radio broadcasts by, 59-60, 62-63, 66-76, 102-13

Murrow, Egbert Roscoe. *See* Murrow, Edward R.

Murrow, Ethel (mother), 19-26, 46, 80, *82*, 143-44, 151

Murrow, Janet (wife), *82, 84, 89-90*, 137-38, 141-44, 150, 162

as broadcaster, 74, 105

dines at White House, 78

and Edward's career, 46, 48, 50-51, 53, 55, 74, 113, 129, 135

and Edward's fame, 126, 139

and Edward's illness and death, 155, 157-59

in Europe, 47-48, 53-55, 74-75, 80, *92*, 105-6, 109-11

meets and marries Edward, 41, 45-46

and Pearl Harbor story, 79

recalls Edward's mother, 20

and *See It Now* McCarthy program, 125, 139-40

Murrow, Janet (*continued*)
  war work done by, 74-75, 77, 105,
    109-10
  on world tour with family, 135-37
Murrow, Lacey (brother), 20-26, 30,
    32, 151
Murrow, Roscoe (father), 19-25, 46,
    80, *82,* 143
Mutual Broadcasting Network, 13

National Education Association, 50
National Student Federation of
    America, 34-41
Nazism, 44-45. *See also* Hitler,
    Adolph; World War II
NBC (National Broadcasting
    Company), 60, 163
Newspapers, 43, 110
  *New York Times* ads for *See It Now,* 1,
    123
  *New York Times* reports on NSFA
    convention, 38-39
North Carolina, Murrow family con-
    nection to, 19, 21, 41, 46

O'Brian, Jack, 12
Ochs, Adolph, 38

Paley, William, xi, 2, 49-50, 58, 63,
    77, 101, 105, 113-14, 133, 138-39
Patton, George, 111
Peabody Award for Excellence in
    Reporting, 113
Peace Corps, 155
Peale, Norman Vincent, 138
Peress, Irving, 7-8
*Person to Person,* 126-29, 142
Phi Beta Kappa, 35

Poland, invasion by Germany of, 63,
    65-66
Powell, Lewis, 34, 36

Race discrimination, 37-39
Radio, 43-44, 59-63, 65, 110, 133-34.
    *See also* Broadcast journalism; *see
    also under* CBS; Murrow, Edward R.
  government-controlled in Europe,
    50, 58
  public affairs programming, 48
  Voice of America, 147
Radio-Television News Directors'
    Association, 133-34, 162
Radulovich, Milo, 2, 122-24
Rather, Dan, 162-63
Red Scare, 121
Reith, John, 55
Rickover, Hyman G., 88
Rockefeller Foundation, 44
Rooney, John J., 152
Roosevelt, Eleanor, 74, 78, 128
Roosevelt, Franklin Delano, 43, 65,
    78-79, 102, 111
Rumblewood, 138
Russia. *See* Soviet Union

Saerchinger, Cesar, 47, 50, 54, 62
Salk, Jonas, 121
Sandburg, Carl, 121, 151
Schlesinger, Arthur, 153
*See It Now,* 1-2, 8-14, 117-26, 128-30,
    134, 145, 162
Senate Government Operations
    Committee, 6
Sevareid, Eric, 60, 161
Shirer, William L., 57-61, 63, 114
Sinatra, Frank, 128
*Small World,* 130, 136

Smith, Howard K., 60, 113
Soviet Union, 2-3, 41, 61, 150, 155
Stokowski, Leopold, 128

Taubman, Howard, 117
Television, 117-18, 121, 133-34. *See
    also* Broadcast journalism; *see also
    under* CBS; Murrow, Edward R.
  live broadcasts, 1, 126-27
  quiz shows, 129, 133-34
  *This I Believe,* 126
  *This . . . Is London,* 66-76, 102, 162
Thomas, Lowell, 138, 143
Trout, Robert, xiii, 49, 59, 113-14,
    163
Truman, Harry, 4, *89,* 129

University of Virginia, 25-26
U.S. Army
  alleged Communist infiltration of,
    7-9, 16-17
  Reserve Officer Training Corps
    (ROTC), 30, 33-34
U.S. Holocaust Memorial Museum,
    161
U.S. Information Agency (USIA),
    147-56
U.S. State Department
  alleged Communist infiltration of,
    3-5, 9-10, 14
  criticizes Murrow, 129

Voice of America, 147-48

Washington (state)
  Beaver, 25
  Blanchard, 21, 25
  Edison, 24
  Murrow family moves to, 21
  Murrow's attachment to, 26-27
  Pullman, 26, 29, 35, 46
Washington State University, 26, 29-
    35, 80
Williams, Chester, 34, 36-37
Willis, Fred, 46-47
Wilson, Donald M., *92,* 148, 150,
    154, 156
World War I, 53
World War II, 63-112
  D day, 108-9
  events leading to, 43-44, 55-65
  and France, 61-62, 69
  and German academics, 44-45, 47-48
  Holocaust, 102-3, 111-12
  and Italy, 62, 79
  and Japan, 78-79
  and McCarthy, Joseph, 5
  and North Africa, 103-4
  Pearl Harbor, 78-79
  and Soviet Union, 2-3, 61
  and United States, 65-66, 75-76, 78-
    80, 101-13

*You Are There,* 113

Zorach, William, 127
Zwicker, Bernard, 7-9